THE ARCHIVE OF THE MISSPELLING OF

GRAHAM FAGEN

THE ENCYCLOPEDIA OF

36
45p

Birds

ALL THE BIRDS OF BRITAIN & EUROPE IN COLOUR

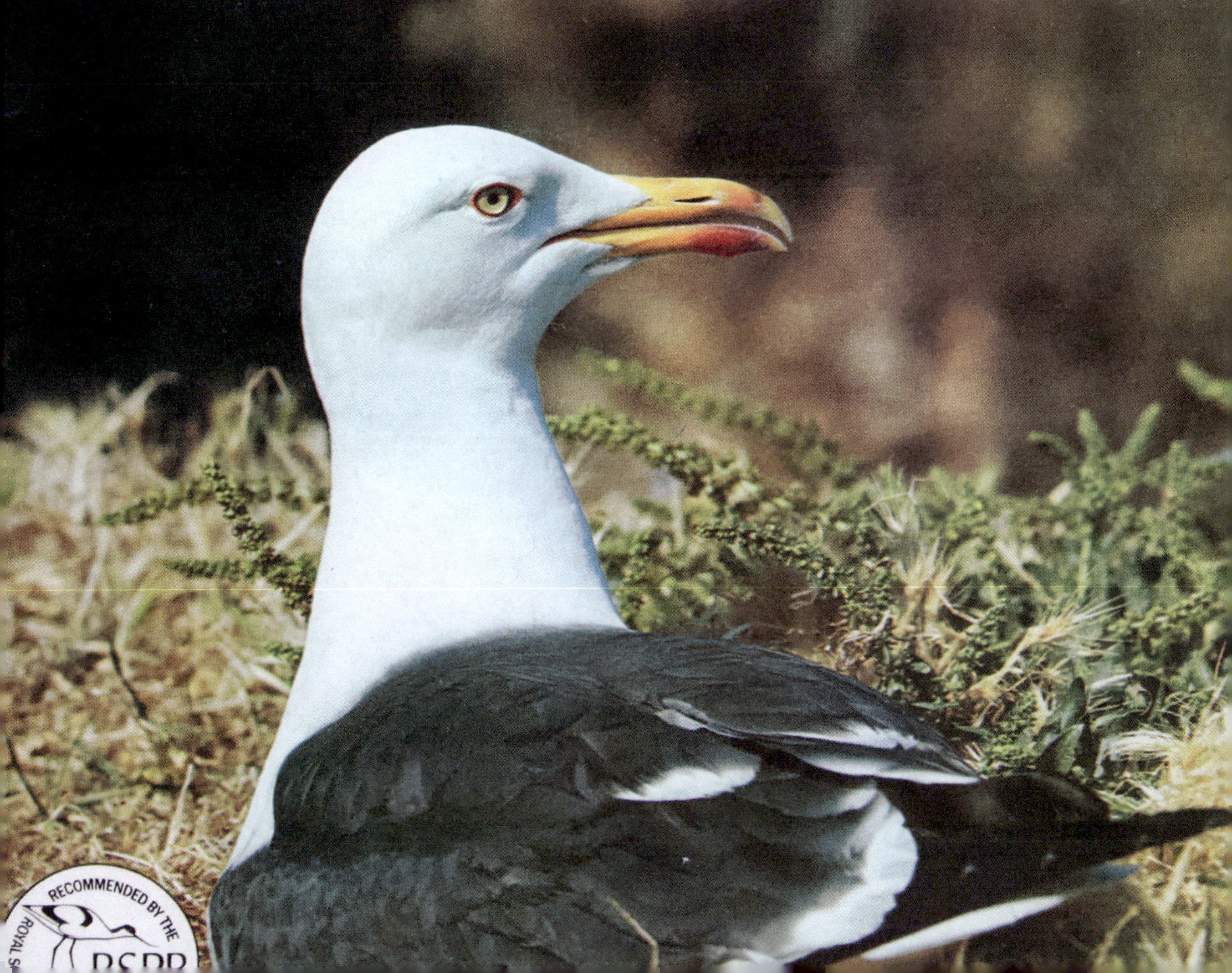

MATT'S GALLERY

92 Webster Road, Bermondsey, London SEI6 4DF
www.mattsgallery.org

9 January 2020

Dear DJCAD Research,

I am writing in support of Graham Fagan's proposed project *Ping Pong Club* to be presented at Queens Park Railway Club as part of Glasgow International, 23 April – 10 May 2020. As part of this project Grahame is proposing to produce a publication. We are delighted that he asked us to act as publisher for this book.

Matt's Gallery was founded in 1979 and produced its first publication, with artist Jaroslaw Kozlowski in 1980. Since then we have worked with many artists including Brian Catling, Willie Doherty, Susan Hiller and Imogen Stidworthy, to produce a range of different kinds of publications. These have included artist's books, catalogues, monographs and free booklets for exhibitions. Our publications are distributed nationally through Cornerhouse.

Ping Pong Club is a project that naturally lends itself to manifesting in book form; Graham Fagen's collection of misspellings of his own name is both amusing and irritating in the way that the best conceptual art is. We hope that Duncan of Jordanstone College of Art & Design will support the realisation of this project.

Sincerely,

Robin Klassnik OBE
Founder and Director
Matt's Gallery
robin.klassnik@mattsgallery.org

T (020) 7237 0398   E info@mattsgallery.org

Director: Robin Klassnik
Registered Charity No.II69683   Company No.I0231860   VAT No.697I5I405

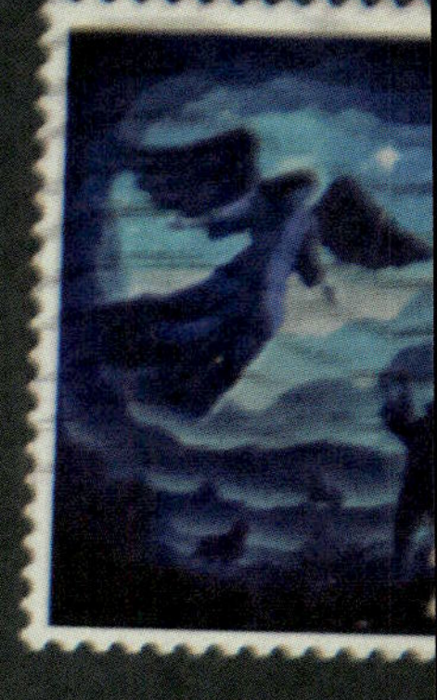

TO MR. MRS G. FAGAN ~ Family

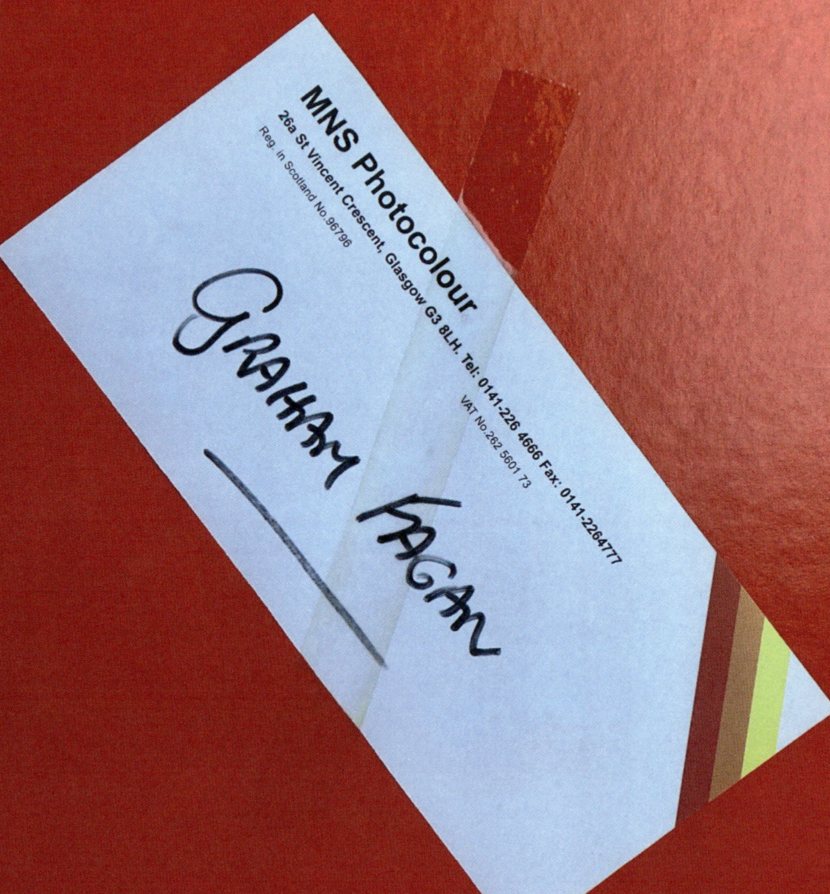

MNS Photocolour
26a St Vincent Crescent, Glasgow G3 8LH. Tel: 0141-226 4666 Fax: 0141-2264777
Reg. in Scotland No.96798
VAT No.262 5601 73

GRAHAM FAGAN

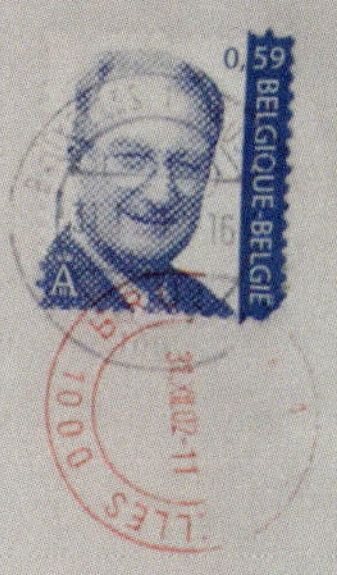

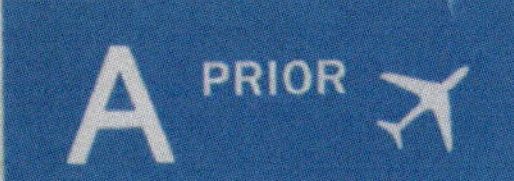

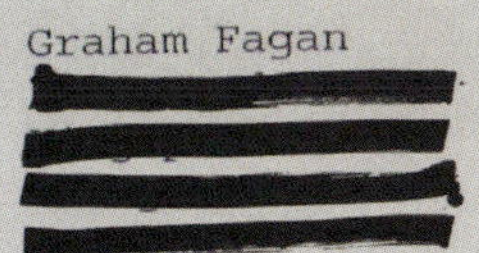

Bruxelles, December 31st, 2002.

Dear Graham,

never again, for the last time.

Yours,

Douglas Gordon.

Graham
Fagan
CAP

Crawford Building
School of Art & Design
University of Dundee

GRAHAM FAGAN
2/R
14 McLENNAN STREET
MOUNT FLORIDA
GLASGOW
G42 9DQ.

Proforma Invoice

Airbill number 7985-4249-2824   **Date of export 06.21.12**

SHIPPER / EXPORTER	CONSIGNEE
CHAD DAWKINS ARTPACE 445 NORTH MAIN AVE. SAN ANTONIO, TX 78205 USA 210-212-4900	Graham Fagan

		CONTACT ON BEHALF OF CONSIGNEE
COUNTRY OF EXPORT	USA	
COUNTRY OF MANUFACTURE	USA	
COUNTRY OF FINAL DESTINATION	UK	
NUMBER OF PACKAGES	1	
TERMS AND PAYMENT	**NO SALE**	
TOTAL VALUE	853.00 USD	

NO SALE. RETURN OF ARTIST'S PERSONAL MATERIALS.

ITEM	DESCRIPTION	SIZE	WEIGHT	VALUE
box contents	1 set of bronze teeth with ebony stand attached		LBS	350.00 USD
	9 sets of bronze teeth			300.00 USD
	2 pieces milled and prepared ebony wood			25.00 USD
	6 pieces of cast bronze rod			5.00 USD
	10 sets of bronze hinges			5.00 USD
	30 pieces bronze welding rod			25.00 USD
	1 WD Live TV Plus media player			100.00 USD
	1 USB drive with video file			5.00 USD
	1 plastic mould of teeth			5.00 USD
	2 sets clear plastic teeth			5.00 USD
	1 set wax teeth on metal dental armature			20.00 USD
	6 drill bits			6.00 USD
	1 vinyl record			1.00 USD
	1 paperback book			1.00 USD

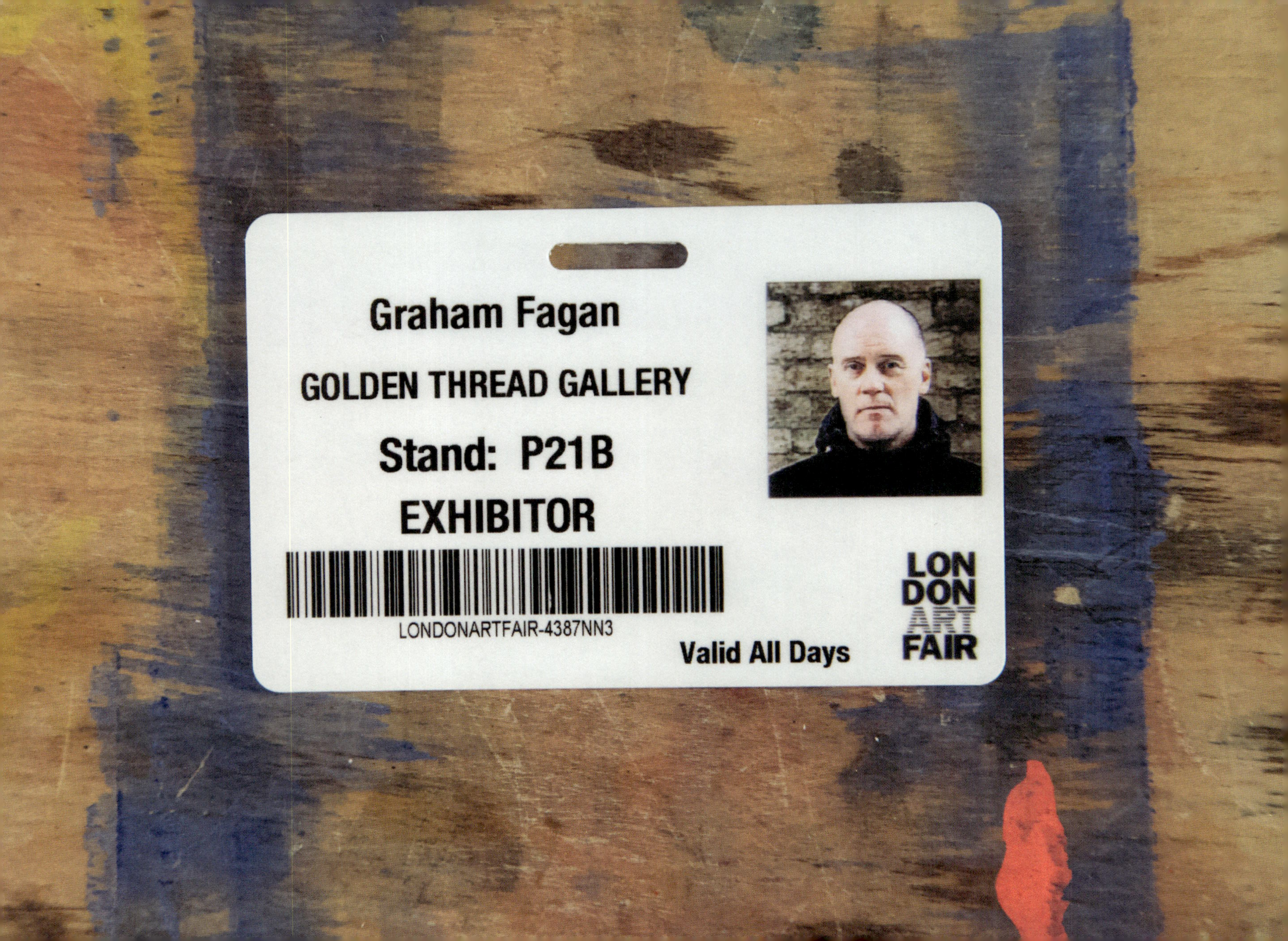
Graham Fagan
GOLDEN THREAD GALLERY
Stand: P21B
EXHIBITOR
LONDONARTFAIR-4387NN3
Valid All Days
LON
DON
ART
FAIR

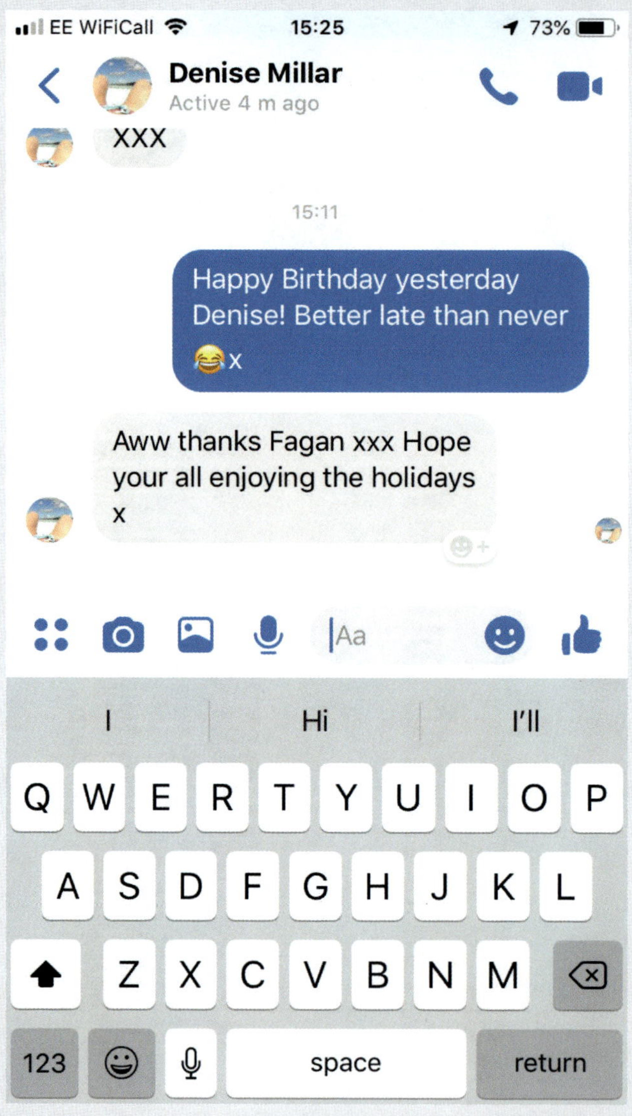
EE WiFiCall   15:25   73%
Denise Millar
Active 4 m ago
XXX
15:11
Happy Birthday yesterday Denise! Better late than never 😂 x
Aww thanks Fagan xxx Hope your all enjoying the holidays x
Aa
I   Hi   I'll
Q W E R T Y U I O P
A S D F G H J K L
Z X C V B N M
123   space   return

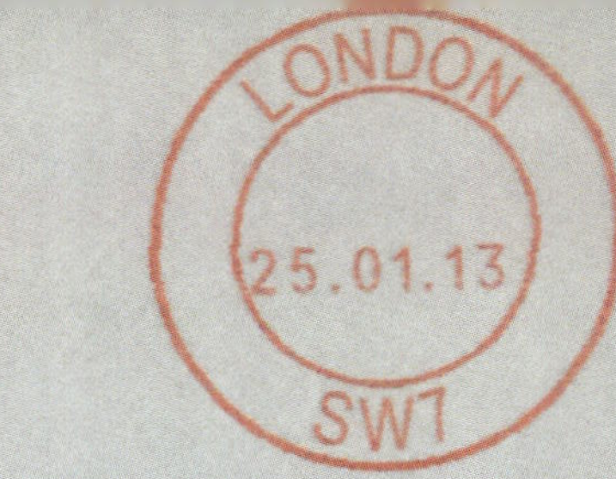

175
Royal College of Art

LONDON
25.01.13
SW1

Graham Fagan
Duncan of Jordanstone College
Fine Art
Perth Road
Dundee
DD1 4HT

Receipt

COLLECT FROM

Graham Fagen
2/R 14 McLennan Street
Mount Florida
Glasgow G42 9DQ

TEL   0141 632 9847

sb.

Owner

Graham Fagan, Glasgow

Exhibition

British Art Show 5 >

Artist, Title, Media, Dimensions	Comments

parts of a work by GRAHAM FAGEN
Nothank, 1999
4. plants + research materials (only)

+ 6 works by GRAHAM FAGEN
Weapons (Blow Pipe), 1998
Cibachrome print, text; 61 x 50.8 cm

Weapons (Crossbow), 1998
Cibachrome print, text; 61 x 50.8 cm

Weapons (Finger Sling), 1998
Cibachrome print, text; 61 x 50.8 cm

Weapons (Flame Thrower), 1998
Cibachrome print, text; 61 x 50.8 cm

Weapons (Petrol Bomb), 1998
Cibachrome print, text; 61 x 50.8 cm

Weapons (Pish Balloon), 1998
Cibachrome print, text. 61 x 50.8 cm

<   **Wrap & pack into 3 MDF crates:-**
18 x 79 x 60 cm (3 Weapons photos)
18 x 79 x 60 cm (3 Weapons photos)
21 x 33 x 27 cm (clip frames) X 6

mr. G. Fagin.

RE ADDRESS

Please
forward.

GRAHAM FAGEN
14 McLENNAN ST
MT. FLORIDA
GLASGOW.

Graham Fagin Esq

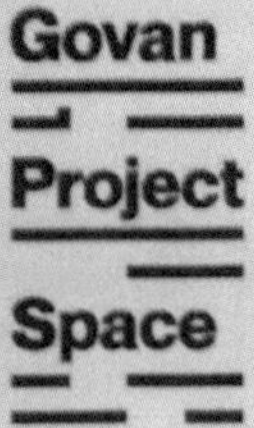

NEXT TOP MODEL

Gwen Dupre

This work comes out of a research project that has been looking at the Pollok Free State activist camp, a group who stood against the routing of the M77 through Pollok Park in the early 1990's. The work uses mud from the original site of the camp which has been cast using a mould from a horse shoe found on a walk in Dumfries and Galloway; it is displayed here along with a sketchbook extract.

Graham Fagan

this should be Roddy Buchanan

I've wanted to make this since 2007. The date's stuck in my head because I remember having a conversation with this man at the opening of my exhibition 'From a City of One Million' at La Criee in Rennes. We talked about the risks you can take in a museum and I said I'd always wanted to place a cut-throat razor on a plinth in a gallery open to the public. The next day he came into the exhibition with his grandfather's open-razor and said 'I've wondered what to do with this for years - Here, you should have it'. I've always had a visceral response when thinking about open razors, perhaps it goes back to seeing that photograph of George Johnston defending himself against Brian Stewart in the Express back in the 70's. The young guy slashing the old guy in Glasgow city centre. This guilty object has sat in my studio for years. To be true to the intention of the work, as it was discussed all those years ago, the object has to lay unsecured and open to the audience on top of the plinth.

Kenny Hunter

Before the discovery of Australia, the people of Europe were convinced with an unshakable belief that all Swans were white, this was confirmed by all the surrounding evidence. In fact the phrase 'black swan' was a common expression as a statement of the impossible. The discovery of Black Swans in 1697 invalidated this long held belief and illustrates the limitations of our learning from observation and the fragility of our knowledge.

Taking inspiration from this the writer Nassim Nicholas Taleb coined the phrase 'Black Swan Theory' using it to describe any event that is unexpected and has extreme impact, from the success of ideas and religions, to the dynamics of historical events, fashion, art movements and to many elements of our personal lives.

Becky Sik

A homage to paramnesia. 1:20 scale model of the Display Case that the Apollo 10 (a scoping mission and dress rehearsal for the first and only moon landing) was housed in when it was exhibited in Glasgow from August 11- August 16 1971. In the six days the

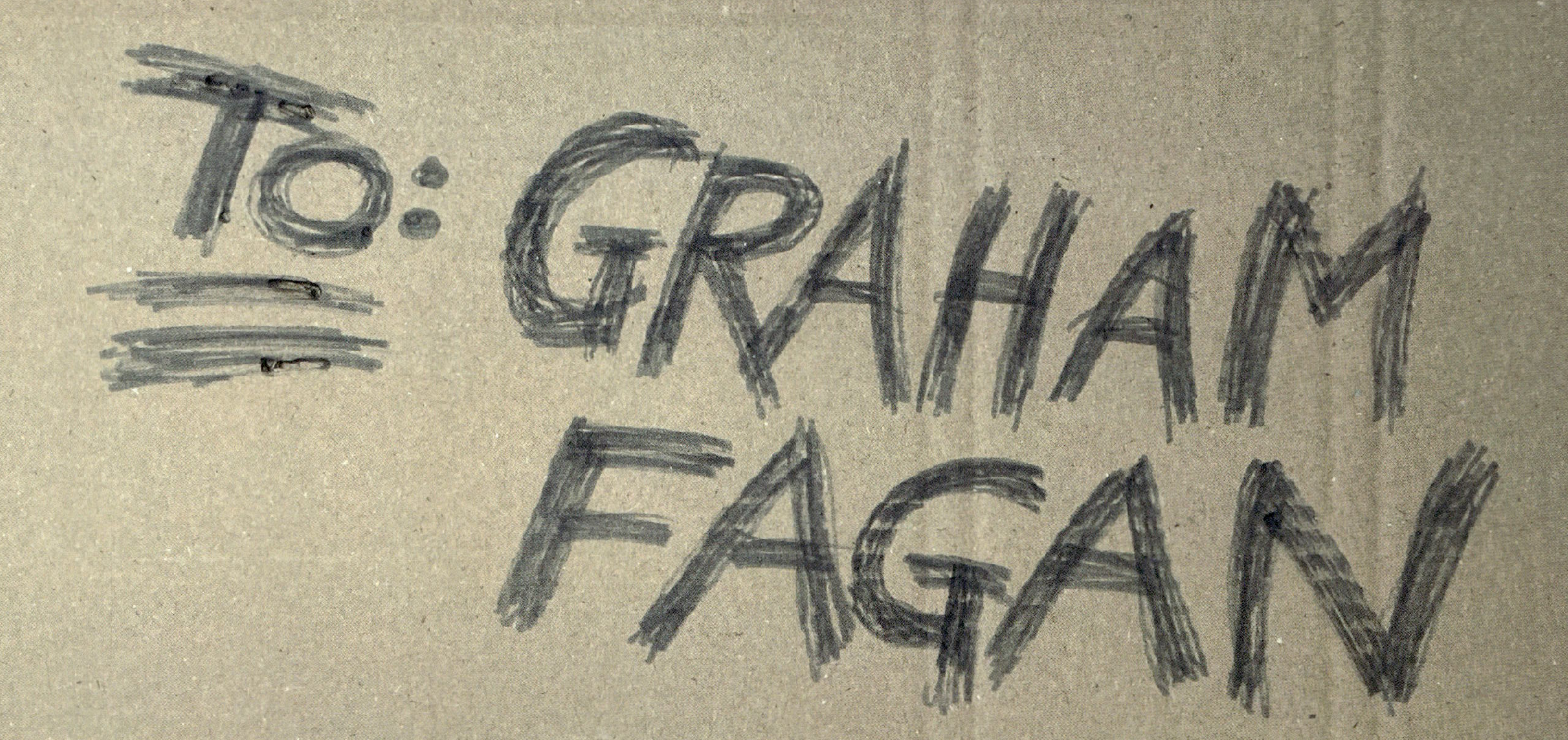

FRAGILE
To: GRAHAM FAGAN
FRAGILE

Art Lending Library
ARTIST
GRAHAM FAGAN
Nº YEL 004
TITLE
MY FAVOURITE FLOWER IS THE PANSY

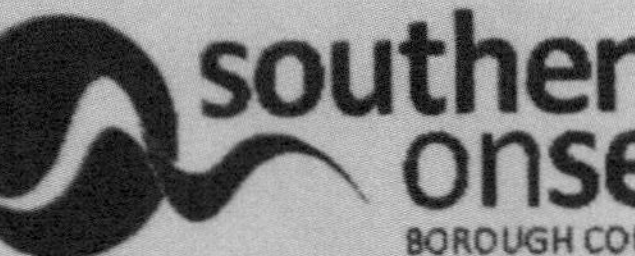

Return Address
Civic Centre Victoria Avenue
Southend On Sea   SS2 6ER

0
5
6
6
6
3
0

Graham Fagan

IWM SE1 6HZ

Graham Fagan

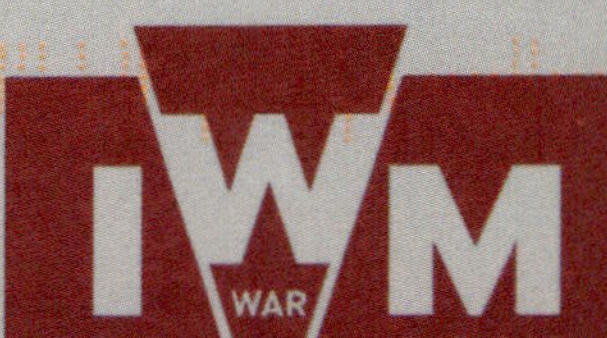

GRAEHAM

FAUEN.

Diane Lees FMA FRSA
Director-General, Imperial War Museums
requests the pleasure of the company of

Graham Fagan

at a reception to mark the opening of IWM London's

FIRST WORLD WAR GALLERIES AND NEW ATRIUM

Thursday 17 July 2014
7pm to 10.30pm

IWM London, Lambeth Road, London SE1 6HZ

Guests will also have the opportunity to visit our new art exhibitions
Truth and Memory: British Art of the First World War and
IWM Contemporary: Mark Neville

RSVP by Thursday 19 June
Helen Blakeborough
launch@iwm.org.uk
020 7416 5394

Dress code: Lounge suit
This invitation card is
strictly non-transferable

Champagne kindly provided by
CHAMPAGNE
POL ROGER

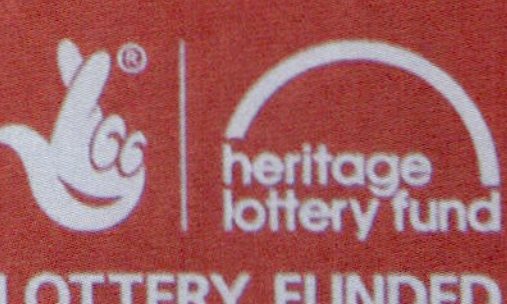

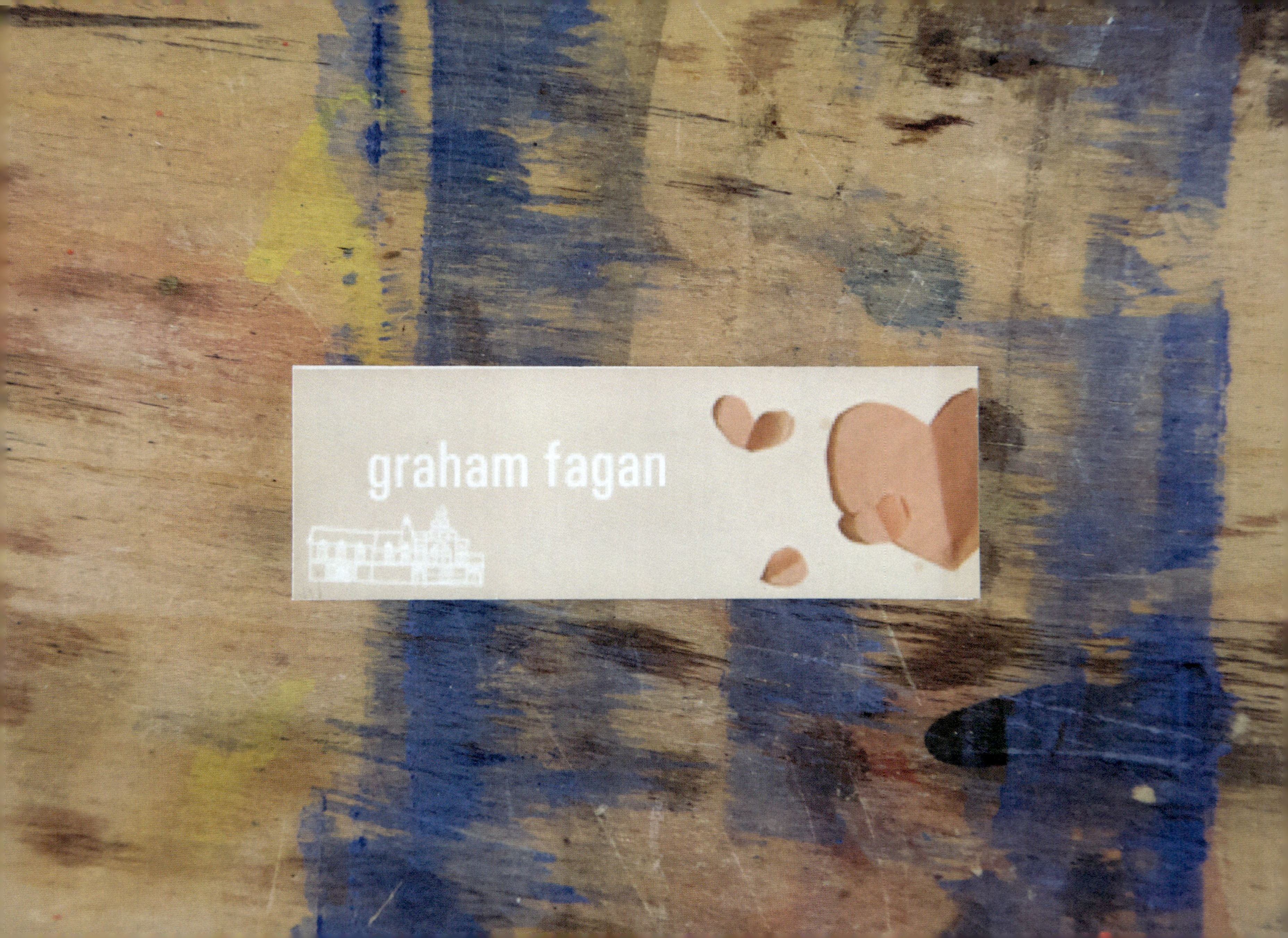

graham fagan

FAGAN BOOK

18 COPIES

NATIONAL GALLERIES OF SCOTLAND

REGISTRAR'S DEPARTMENT

SCOTTISH NATIONAL GALLERY OF MODERN ART, BELFORD ROAD, EDINBURGH, EH4

FAX NUMBER: 0131 332 4939   TELEPHONE NUMBER: 0131 624 6313

EMAIL ADDRESS: jslater@nationalgalleries.org

FAX TRANSMISSION

TO: GRAHAM FAGAN   **FROM:** JANICE SLATER

ADDRESS: GLASGOW   **DEPT:** REGISTRAR'S

DATE: 11 JULY 02

NUMBER OF PAGES ATTACHED INCLUDING COVER: (

Please phone immediately on the above number if any document is illegible or if any papers are missing.

Dear Graham

LOAN OF PORTRAIT OF PRINCE CHARLES EDWARD STUART

Following our telephone conversation earlier, I checked our paperwork. At the moment the loan is still pending. A letter was sent to Dr Vittorio Urbani on 6 May requesting further details about security and environmental arrangements at the ICI, and further information on the exhibition and its content. Another letter requesting information on facilities and security was sent to Mario Fortunato on 18 June (enclosing a facilities questionnaire). I'm afraid we can't make a decision on whether to lend until we receive this information.

In the meantime, the costs are likely to be c. £30 - £50 for glazing, and £295 plus VAT for the hire of the case in which we transport the painting. On top of this the ICI will have to insure the painting and arrange appropriate transport. Fine Art transport can be pretty expensive. As this painting is quite small it's likely one of our staff would 'hand-carry' this to London by air involving two or three airline seats — paintings cannot travel in the hold as there are currently no palletized freight flights between Edinburgh and London. The courier would also require one nights hotel accommodation and two days subsistence at £35 - £40 per day. These are all standard costs for loans between UK institutions.

We look forward to receiving further information on security, and environmental conditions soon. In the meantime, please don't hesitate to contact us if you need any further information at this stage.

Kind regards

Graham Fagin,
2/R,
14 McLennan Street,
Mount Florida,
Glasgow.
G42 9DQ

GLASGOW
7 45PM
5 JLY
2000
CA

G. Fagin
21R McLen
Mount Floric
Glasgow.
G42 9D

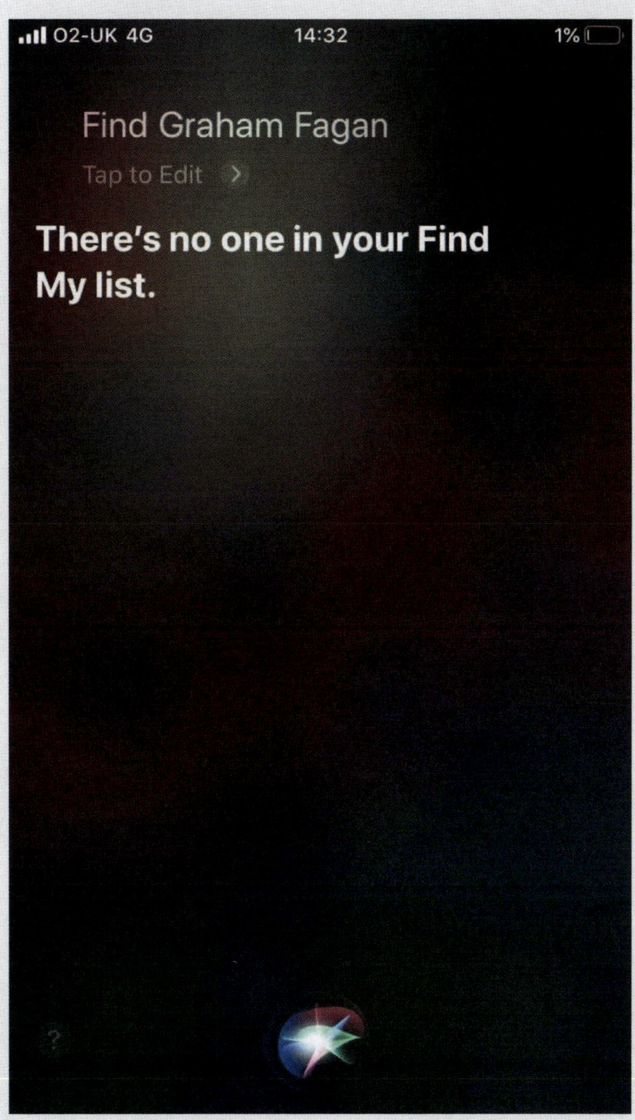
O2-UK 4G
14:32
1%
Find Graham Fagan
Tap to Edit
There's no one in your Find My list.
?

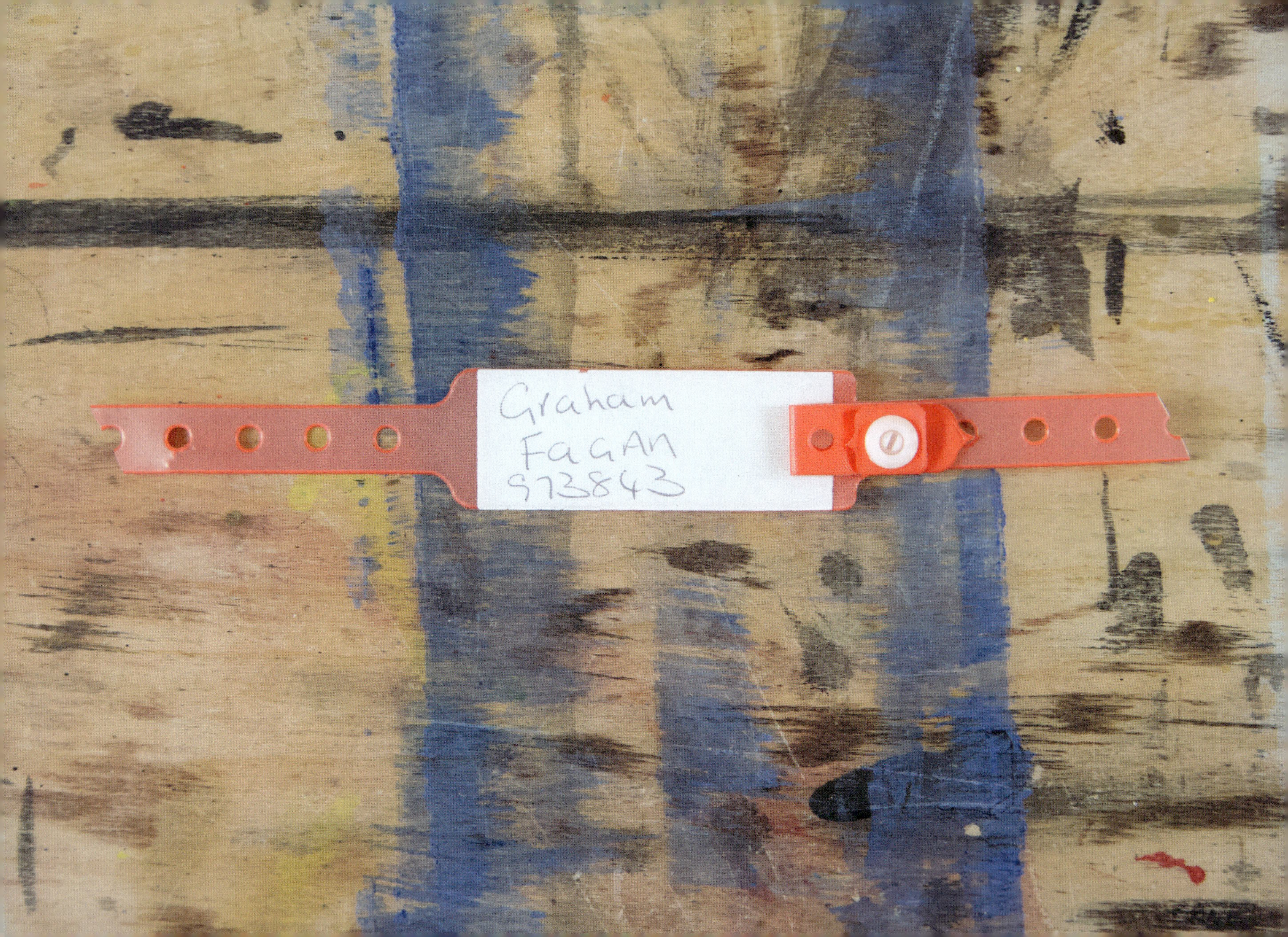

Graham
Fagan
S73843

LEIPZIGER MESSE

BRI... 21.-7.00

'10

G. Fagan
14 Mc Lennan St.
Mount Florida
Glasgow G42
Schottland

Dear Graeme
Apologies. There was payment on 1 November with the reference GF which I have wrongly attributed to another RSA member with the same initials. Your subs are indeed up to date.
Kind regards
Gail

Gail Gray
Finance Administrator
Royal Scottish Academy of Art & Architecture
The Mound, Edinburgh, EH2 2EL.
Tel: 0131 624 6112
www.royalscottishacademy.org
Join the RSA on Facebook
Join the RSA E-Newsletter

____

The RSA is an independently funded institution led by eminent artists and architects to promote and support the creation, understanding and enjoyment of the visual arts. To find out about what we do and how you can become involved tel: 0131 225 6671 or e-mail us.

The RSA is a charity registered in Scotland (No. SC004198), registered address: The RSA, The Mound, Edinburgh, EH2 2EL.

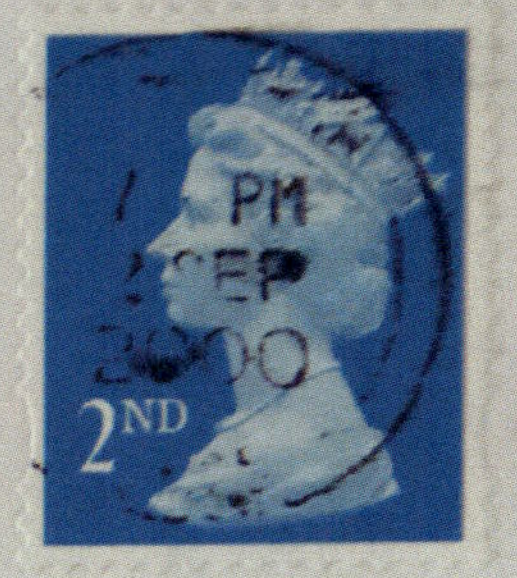

Graham Fagan
14 McLennan Street (2/R)
Mount Florida
Glasgow   G42 9DQ

Mr Graham Fagan
Sculpture Department
Duncan of Jordanstone College

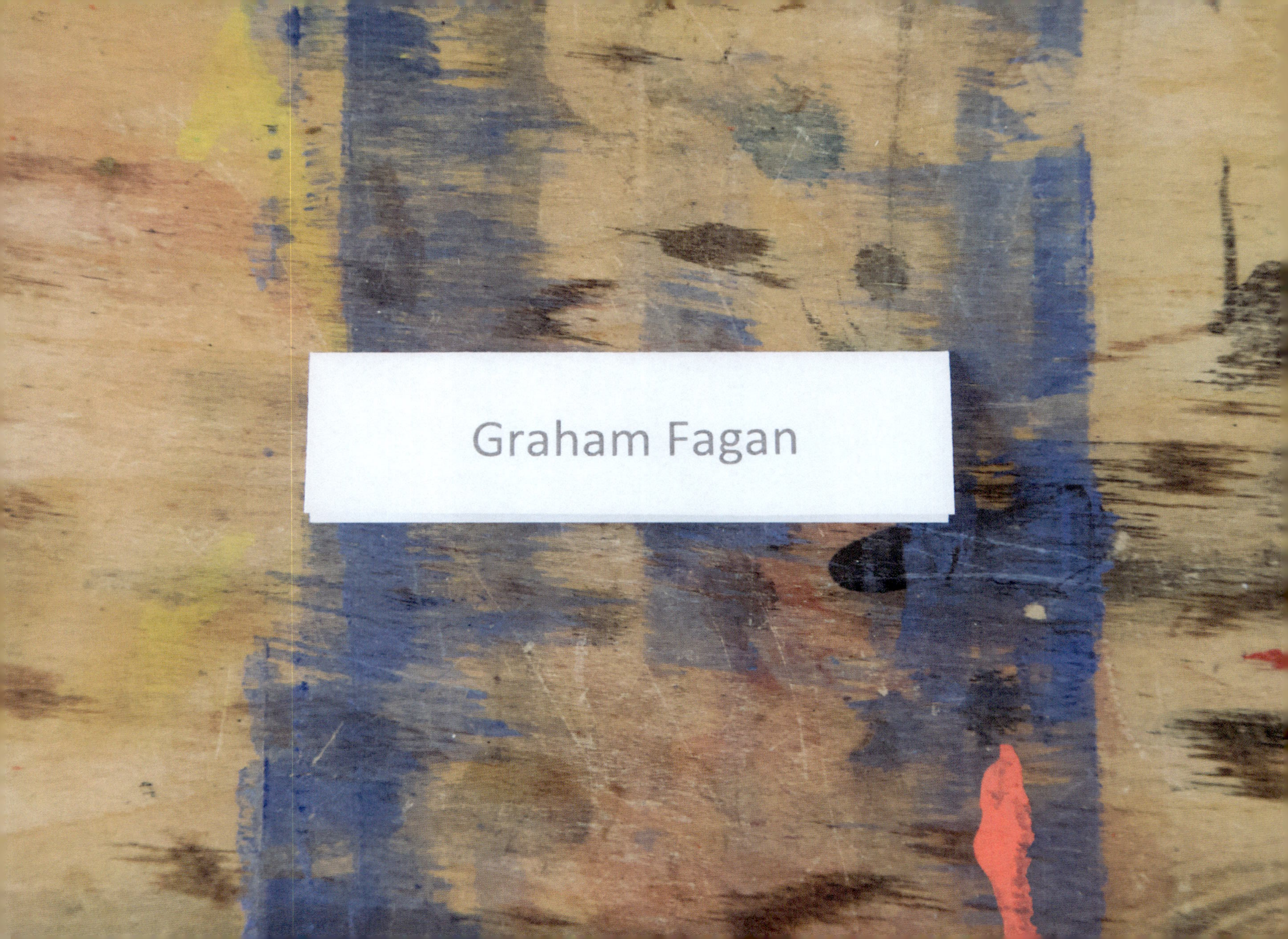
Graham Fagan

SCOTTISH EXECUTIVE

Chief Architect's Office

Victoria Quay
Edinburgh EH6 6QQ

Graham Fagan Esq
Flat 2/2
14 Maclennan Street
Mount Florida
GLASGOW
G42 9DG

Telephone: 0131-244 0774
Fax: 0131-244 7470
architecture@scotland.gov.uk

Your ref:
Our ref:

Date: 16 December 1999

Dear Mr Fagan

OPEN MEETING: A POLICY ON ARCHITECTURE FOR SCOTLAND

As you may know, Rhona Brankin, Scottish Executive Minister with responsibility for architecture, recently launched a consultation document, *The Development of a Policy on Architecture for Scotland.* A copy of the document is enclosed.

As part of the consultation process, a series of open meetings has been planned at locations throughout Scotland. The purpose of the meetings is to canvas the views and comments of as wide a range of interests as possible on the issues set out in the consultation document. I am pleased to invite you to one of these meetings. The meeting will take place at 7.00pm on Tuesday 18 January 2000 at The Lighthouse.

If you are unable to attend the meeting, then please do feel free to pass this invitation on to a colleague. Equally, if you wish to bring along other colleagues who may have an interest, then please do feel free to extend this invitation. As there will be a limit to the numbers that can be accommodated, I would be grateful if you would confirm if you, or other colleagues, will be able to attend.

Yours sincerely

J E GIBBONS
Chief Architect

🏠 About   Visit   2019 exhibition   **Explore our history**   Fellowship opportunities

Home > Explore our history > 2010s

2015 Graham Fagan (Scotland)

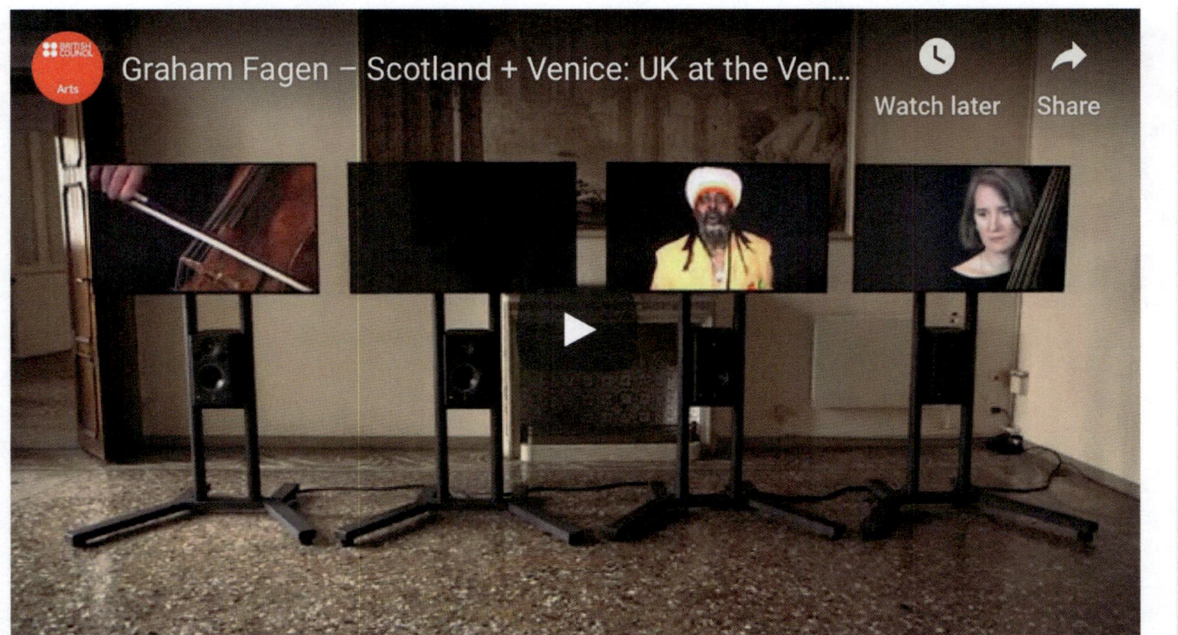

∧ 2010s

2017 Phyllida Barlow

2018 ISLAND

2016 Home Economics

2015 Sarah Lucas

2015 Graham Fagan (Scotland)

2015 Helen Sear (Wales)

Google

graham fagen   ✕

graham fagen the slave's lament 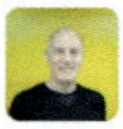
graham fagan artist
Graham Fagen — Scottish artist
graham fagan peterborough
graham fagan aib
graham fagen dundee

Google Search   I'm Feeling Lucky

Report inappropriate predictions

n Her Majesty's Servi

Graham Fagan

VISITOR

422

BBC

WESTERN HOUSE

DATE: 10 MAR 2015

NAME	GRAHAM PAGIN	TIME IN 1530
VISITING	GC	EXTENSION NO. 5103

VALID ON DAY OF ISSUE ONLY. PLEASE RETURN THIS PASS TO RECEPTION

LOCI
design

LANDSCAPE ARCHITECTURE

Fao. Graham Pigin .

WITH COMPLIMENTS

Top Floor
2 Clifton Street
Glasgow
G3 7LA

Tel/Fax: (0141) 353 2288

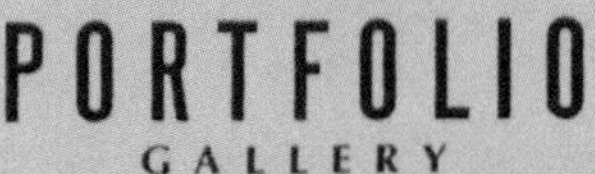

PORTFOLIO
GALLERY

20 October 1999

Graham Fagan
2/R 14 McLennan Street
Mount Florida
GLASGOW
G42 9DQ

Dear Graham

Return of test prints and transparencies

At the request of Matt's Gallery I am returning the following to you:

1. *Weapons*, 1998
    6 transparencies (6x7cm)

2. Plant Series
    7 test prints

Thank you for giving us the chance to look at them.

Yours sincerely

Lesley Young

G. FAGAN

ISIAUES
LAMENT '

MONITOR
STAND
tOOLS .

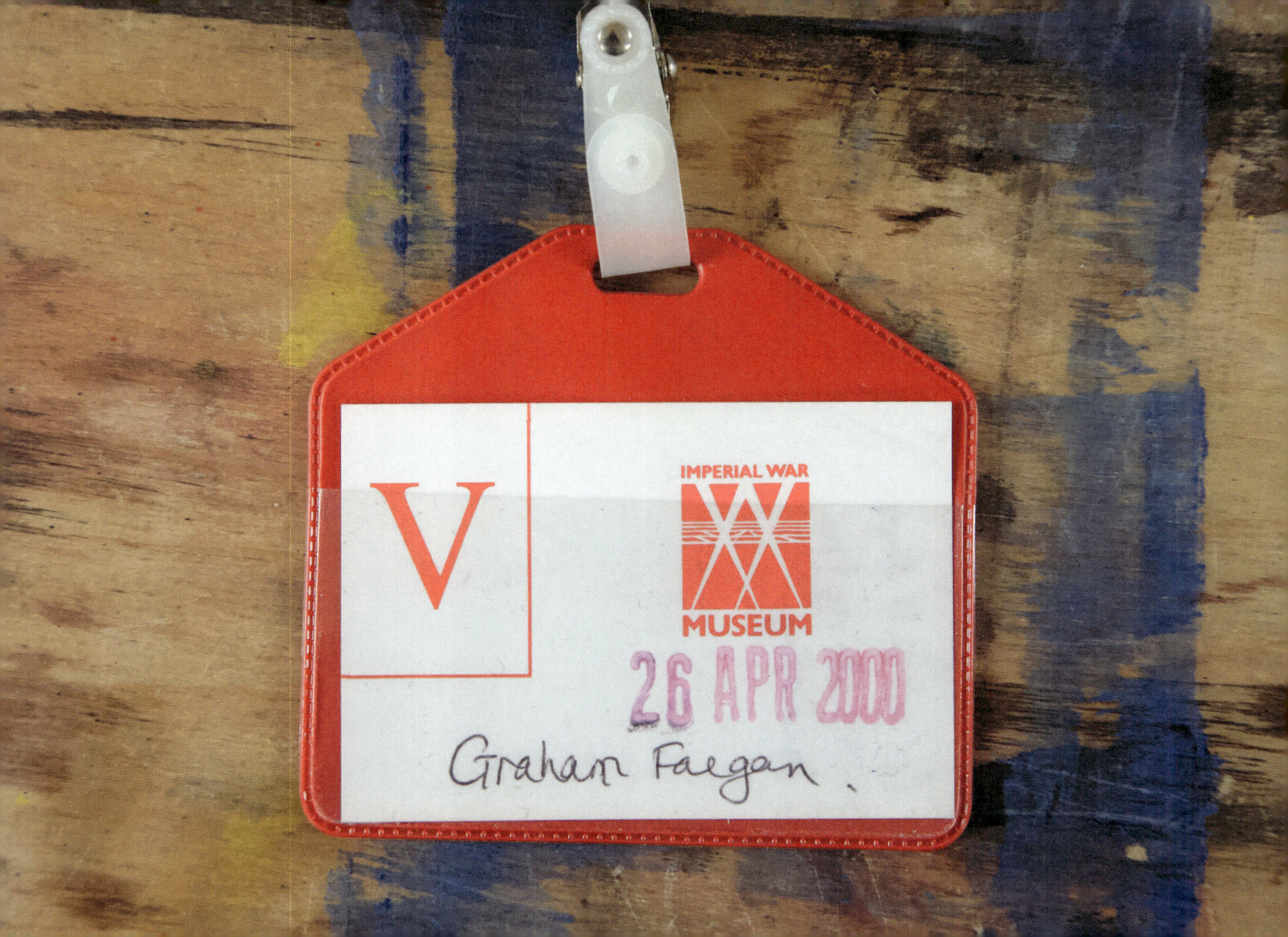

IMPERIAL WAR MUSEUM
26 APR 2000
Graham Faegan
V

50/50 Club MARCH

3rd Prize €5.

G. Fagan.

relocation

an emplacements project
curated by Françoise Dupré and Roxane Permar

18 Museum House
Burnham Street
London E2 OJA

Friday 24th September, 6.00-9.00 pm
Saturday 25th September 1999, 1.00-8.00 pm

Åsa Andersson, Fiona Balfour, Carmel Buckley, Samantha Clark, Françoise Dupré, Graham Fagan, Mark Harris, Sheila Houlston, Leona Johnson, Chris Kool Want, Nayan Kulkarni, Sarat Maharaj, Henna Nadeem, Roxane Permar, Emma Rushton, Karen Scopa, Derek Tyman, work-seth/tallentire.

relocation is the second event in *Emplacements*, the on-going collaborative project initiated by Françoise Dupré and Roxane Permar in l997. **relocation** will take place in an empty flat in a nineteenth century block of purpose built flats. The flat occupies the top two floors in a four-storey building. The building is located in the heart of Bethnal Green in London's East End, situated on the Roman Road and flanked by a fire station and a police station.

With **relocation** artists and writers have been asked to participate at very short notice. This brief period of time reflects the sudden availability of the flat. However, it also mirrors the way in which relocation may occur. **relocation** tests artists' ability and desire to act quickly and flexibly in the spirit of experimentation, participation and collaboration.

The artists and writers represent a variety of backgrounds and generations. The geographical spread and urban versus rural locations of their respective bases provides further diversity to the perspective from which each is working. While the movement between these locations - London, the West Midlands of England, Glasgow, Edinburgh, the Northeast of Scotland and Shetland - reflects the places directly connected to the very personal processes of relocation Dupré and Permar experience, the process speaks of a shared experience that has uniquely emerged in the late twentieth century.

The work in **relocation** embraces the idea of relocation in relation to notions of location and dislocation in a very broad as well as a very particular sense. Works refer to geographical, cultural or metaphorical interpretations of place, space and identity. They focus on physical or topographical qualities. Some works use time in relation to presence and absence. Histories emerge, memories materialise and references to moments of transference appear.

Dupré and Permar set up the project *Emplacments* as a response to their desire to create work flexibly with practitioners who actively engage and respond to critical issues of place, identity and corporality. *Emplacements* explores concerns which are present in Dupre's and Permar's own practices, reflecting their recognition of the complexity of the relationship between the audience, the work and its location. *Emplacements* is an act or an instance of putting in position. *Emplacements* is a situation or a position.

relocation will be included on the Emplacements web site: www.thegallerychannel.com/emplacements

For further details and photographs contact Nancy Proctor at The Gallery Channel:
tel: 0171 379 9220 or email: emplace@thegallerychannel.com

We gratefully acknowledge the support of the following organisations: Gray's School of Art, Robert Gordon University in Aberdeen; Pinkink and The Gallery Channel.

There is no wheelchair access to 18 Museum House.

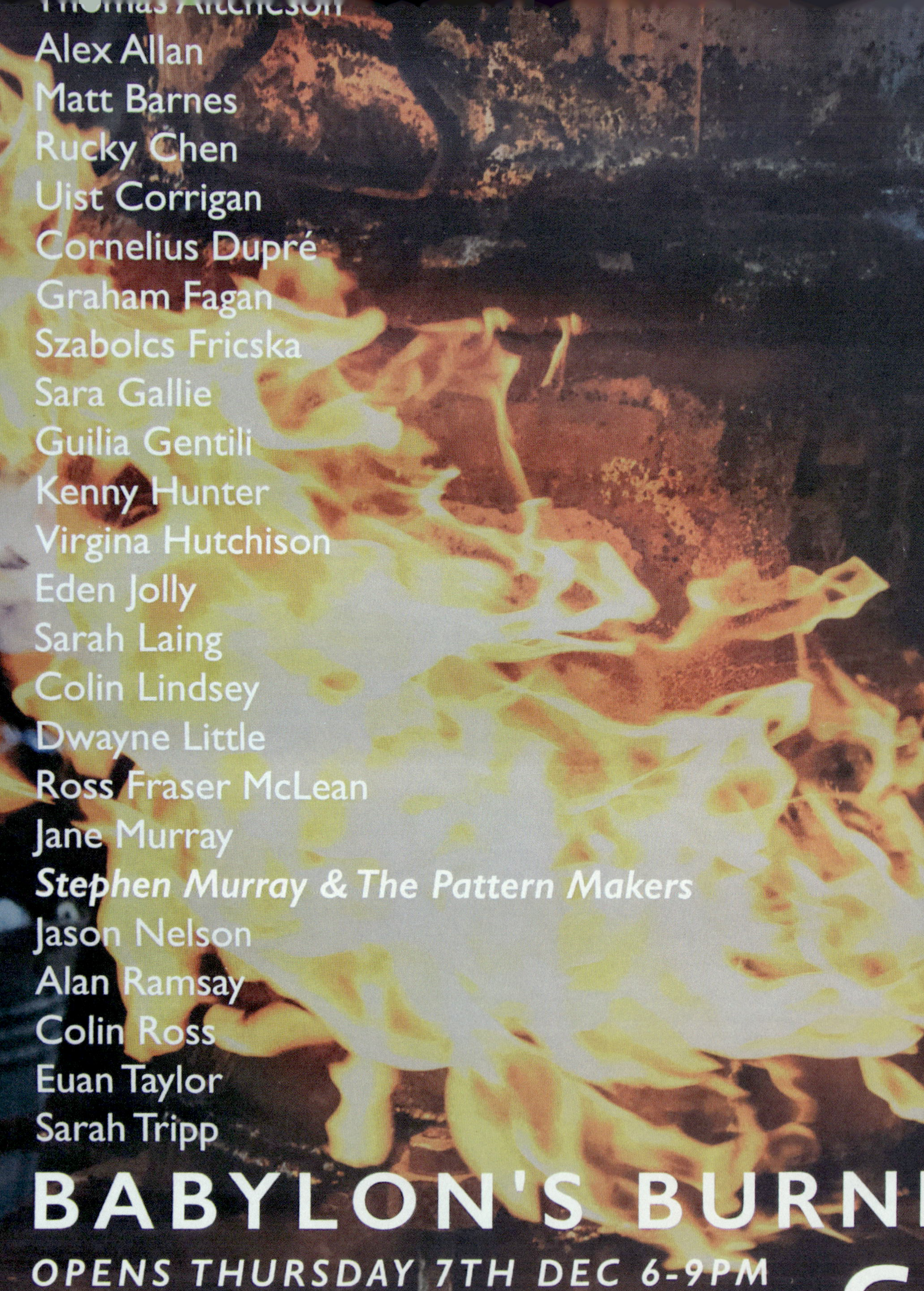

Thomas Aitcheson
Alex Allan
Matt Barnes
Rucky Chen
Uist Corrigan
Cornelius Dupré
Graham Fagan
Szabolcs Fricska
Sara Gallie
Guilia Gentili
Kenny Hunter
Virgina Hutchison
Eden Jolly
Sarah Laing
Colin Lindsey
Dwayne Little
Ross Fraser McLean
Jane Murray
Stephen Murray & The Pattern Makers
Jason Nelson
Alan Ramsay
Colin Ross
Euan Taylor
Sarah Tripp
BABYLON'S BURNI
OPENS THURSDAY 7TH DEC 6-9PM

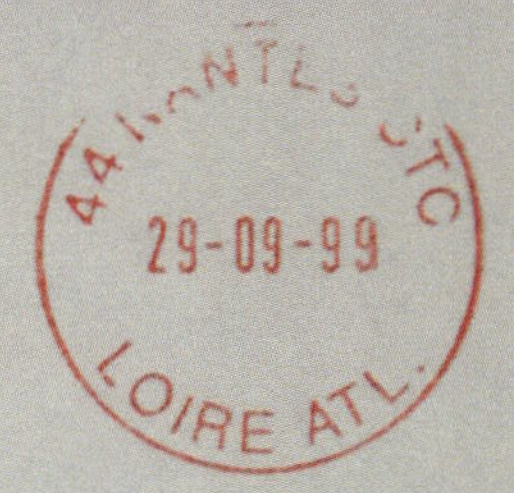

NANTES
MAIRIE

2, rue de l'Hôtel de Ville
44094 NANTES cedex 1
Tél. 02 40 41 90 00 - Fax 02 40 41 92 39
3615 NANTES - http://www.Mairie-Nantes.fr

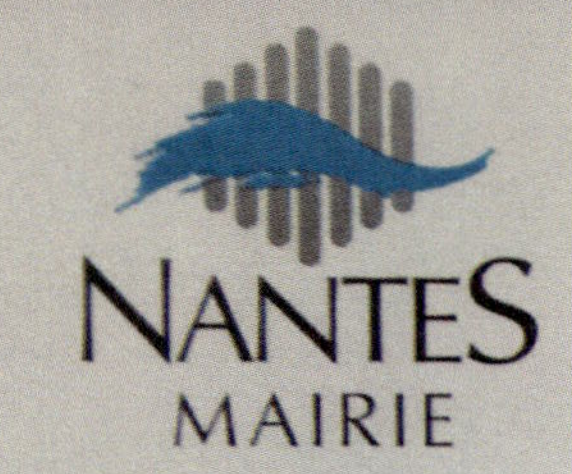

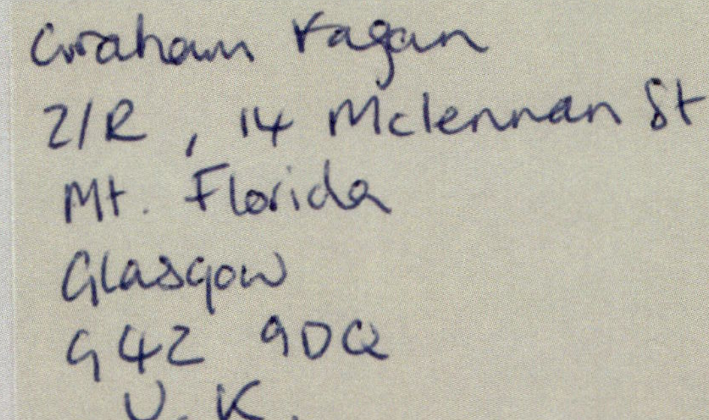

Graham Fagan
21R , 14 Mclennan St
Mt. Florida
Glasgow
G42 9DQ
U.K.

29-09-99
44 NANTES STC
LOIRE ATL.

Receipt

COLLECT FROM   Graham Fagen
2/R 14 McLennan St.
Mount Florida
Glasgow G42 9DQ

TEL   0141 632 9847

Owner   A.C.C.

Exhibition   A.C.C. New Purchases

Artist, Title, Media, Dimensions   Comments

GRAHAM FAGAN
Former and Form 1993
Concrete, wood and g-clamps
60 x 50 cm

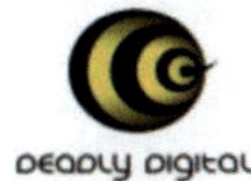

DEADLY DIGITAL LIMITED
WWW.DEADLYDIGITAL.COM

Graham Fagan   £28.50

Total: £28.50

VAT (20%): £4.75

CARD PAYMENT (CONTACTLESS)

VISA *2554

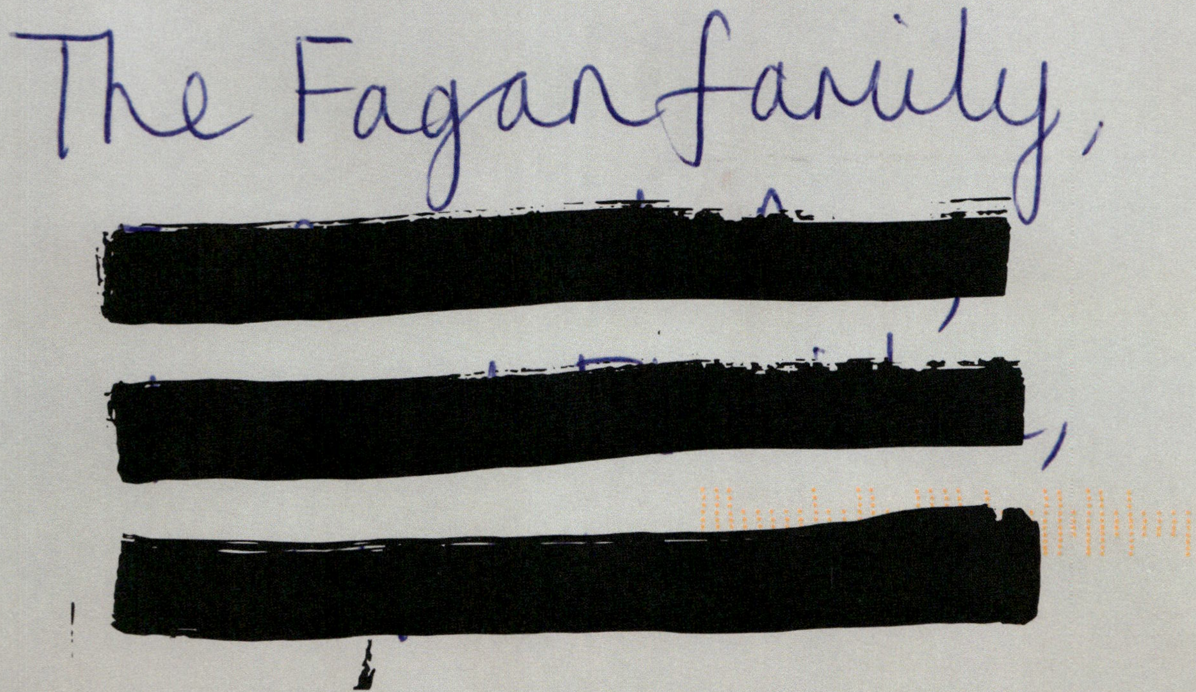

LAST POSTING DATES
2nd class - Wed 18th
1st class - Fri 20th
Special Delivery - Mon 23rd
Royal Mail
Glasgow
Mail Centre
10-12-2019
21110275
2nd
The Fagan family,

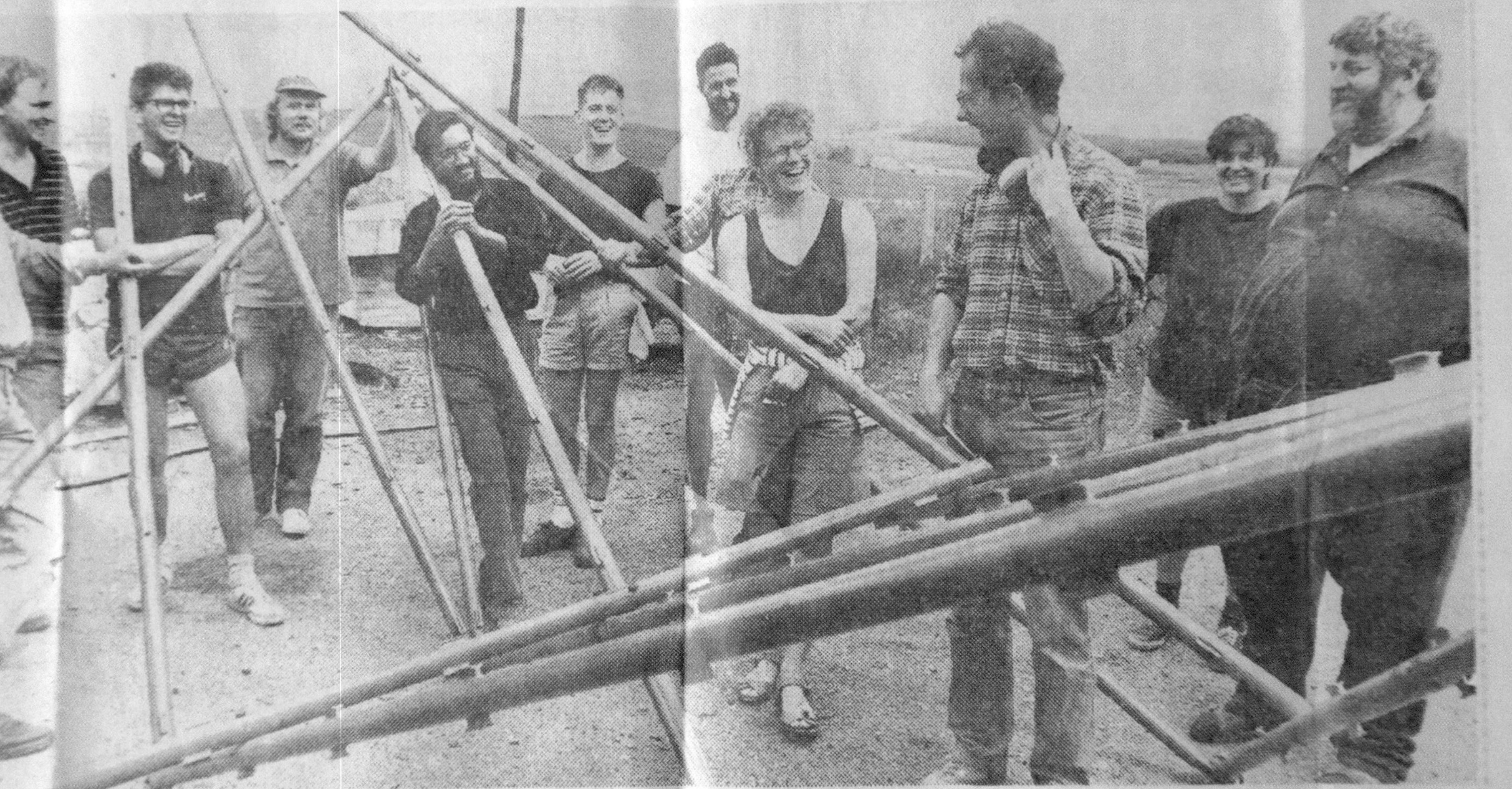

■ Sculptors and their helpers at work at Lumsden (left to right) Perusko Bogdanic, Chris Bailey, Mike Farrell, Ole Sjovold, Pankaj Panwar, Graeme Fagan, Peter Smith, Ann Bovey, Guillaume De La Chaelle, Anne Nicholson and Fred Bushe.

Eurostudents' places to stay

is getting desperate — next month,

Sculpture taking shape at Lumsden has been given international touch

ATLAS

TALKING ART SERIES

EALAN / DAOINE / ÀITE **ART / PEOPLE / PLACE**

www.atlasarts.org.uk

CHRIS DOOKS

Chris Dooks is an audiovisual artist and a composer of electronic music and sound art. Dooks worked in television as a director of arts programmes until 1998, when he fell ill with M.E. He describes coping with chronic ill health and his return to his training as a photographer and his development of a successful art practice.

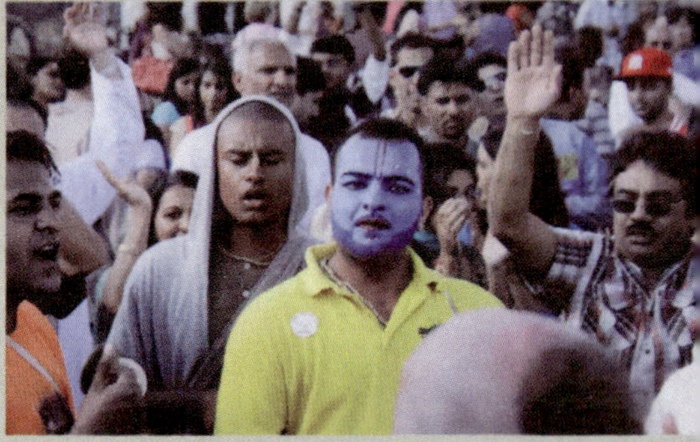
Lens based work from the Hari Krishna project...seeing shapes in chaos © Chris Dooks

GRAHAM FAGAN

Graham Fagan's work Baile an Or follows the cyclical path of the river to the sea in Helmsdale and the Strath of Kildonan. He explores the formation of identity using sculpture, lens based media, text and performance. Fagan has exhibited internationally throughout his career and was invited by the Imperial War Museum, London to work as the Official War Artist for Kosovo.

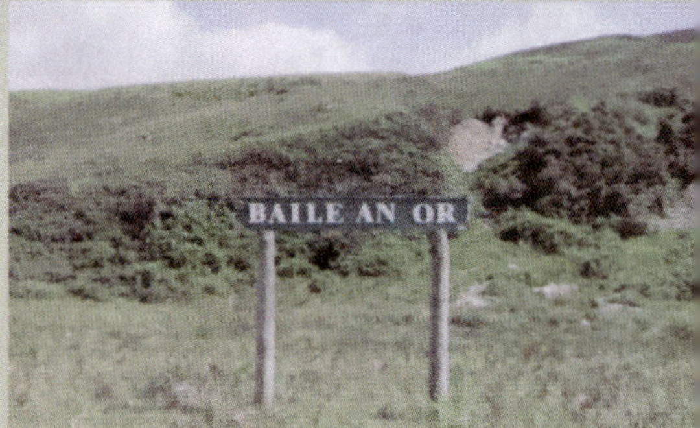

Baile an Or ©Graham Fagan

NICKY BIRD

Nicky Bird presents her work and experience in new media in particular her recent project Archaeology of the Ordinary. Her work investigates the contemporary relevance of found photographs, the hidden histories of archives and specific sites. Since her practice-led PhD

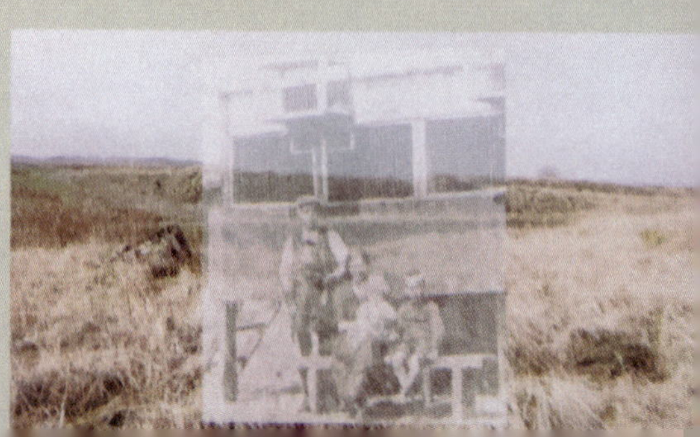

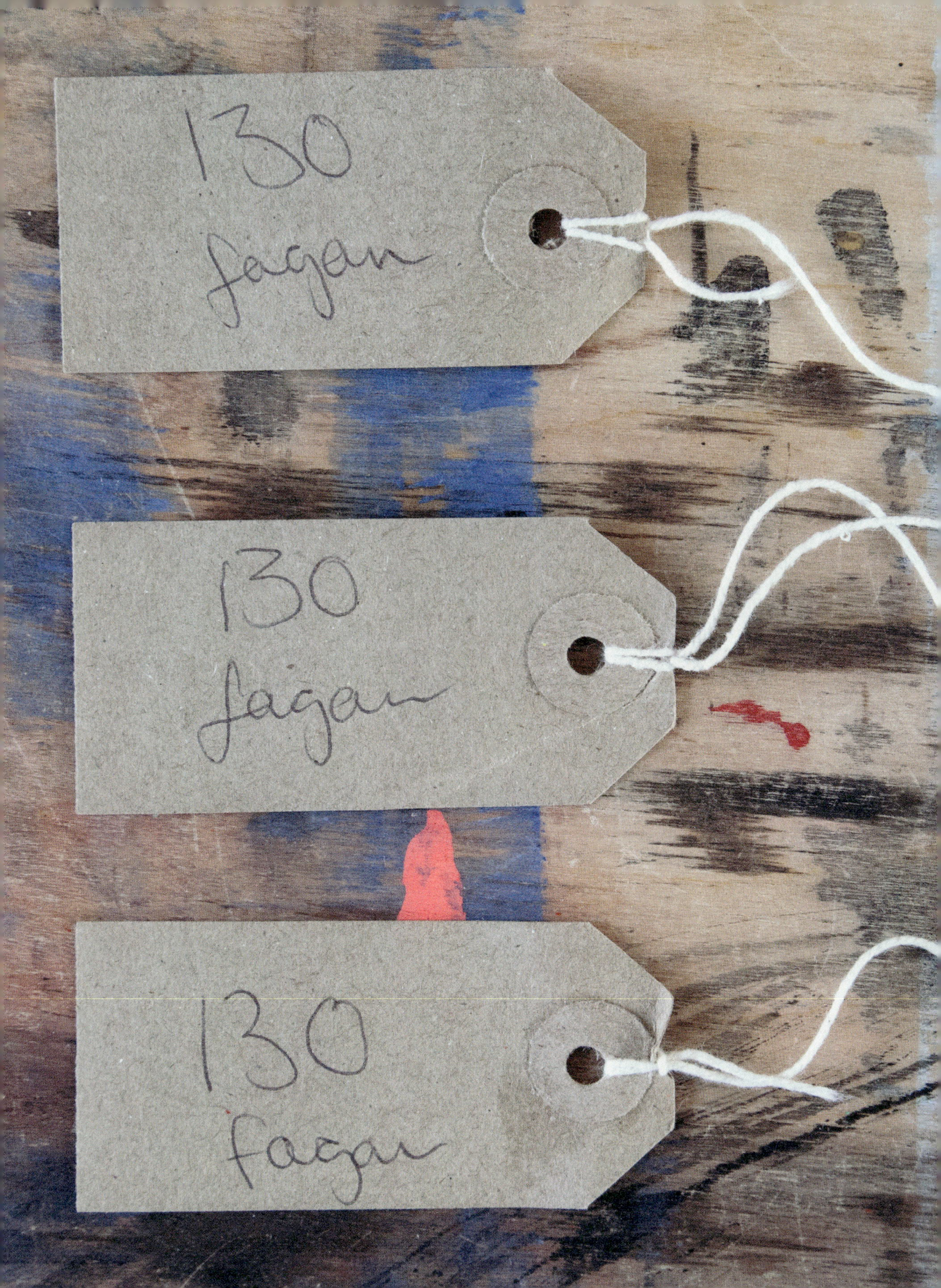
130
fagan
130
fagan
130
fagan

HiscoxCollection

« Back

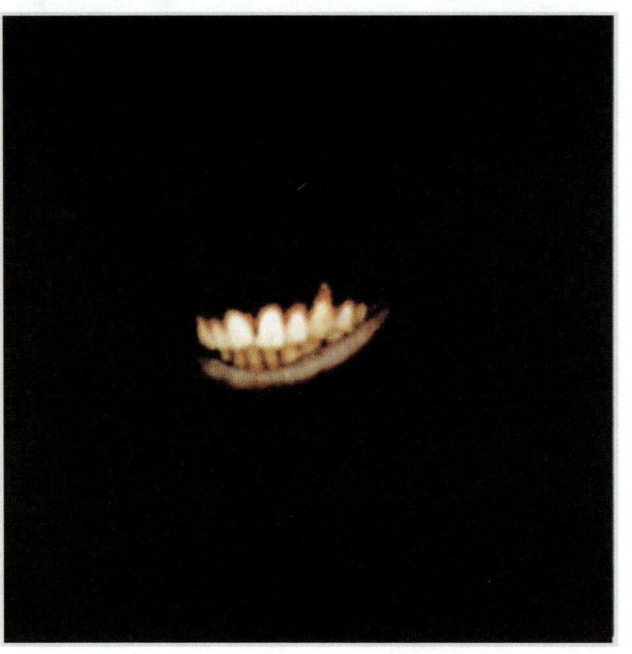

Graham Fagan

My mouth shall speak of wisdom

Year made: 2006

Graham Fagen was born in Glasgow in 1966 where he now lives and works. Fagen studied at the Glasgow School of Art and the Kent Institute of Art and Design. Much of Fagen's work concentrates on identity and communication within divergent cultures. He is interested in how the meanings behind cultural communication change when taken out of context.

Location: London
Date acquired: 12 March 2007

« Back

Privacy Policy | Cookie Policy | Corporate | Terms & Conditions

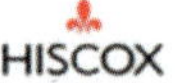
HISCOX

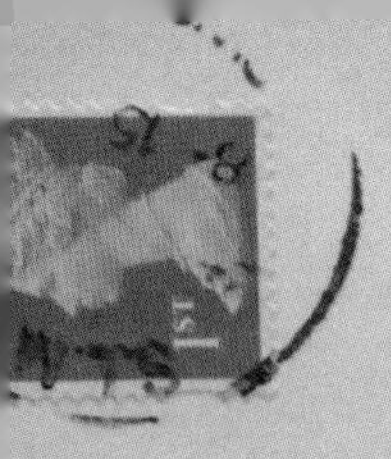
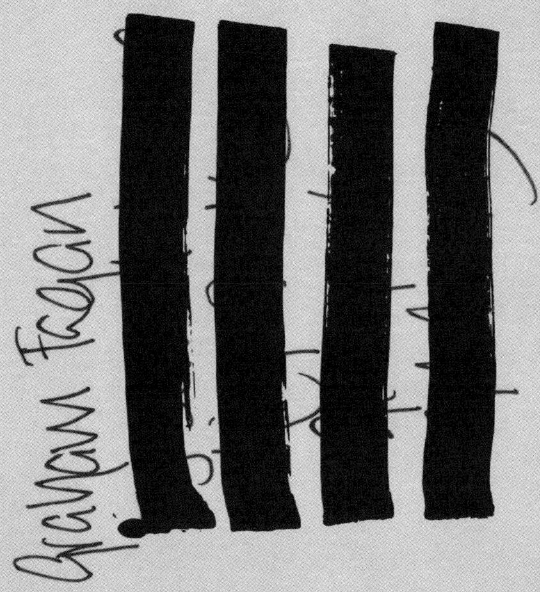
Graham Fagen

THE FLEMING COLLECTION

13 Berkeley Street • London W1J 8DU
Tel 020 7042 5730 www.flemingcollection.com

GRAHAM FASAN —
WEST COAST LOOKING
WEST

Last chances to post:
1st Class -
Friday 20th
Special Delivery -
Monday 23rd

Glasgow
Mail Centre
19-12-2019
20107690

1st

Mr. + Mrs. G. Fagan,

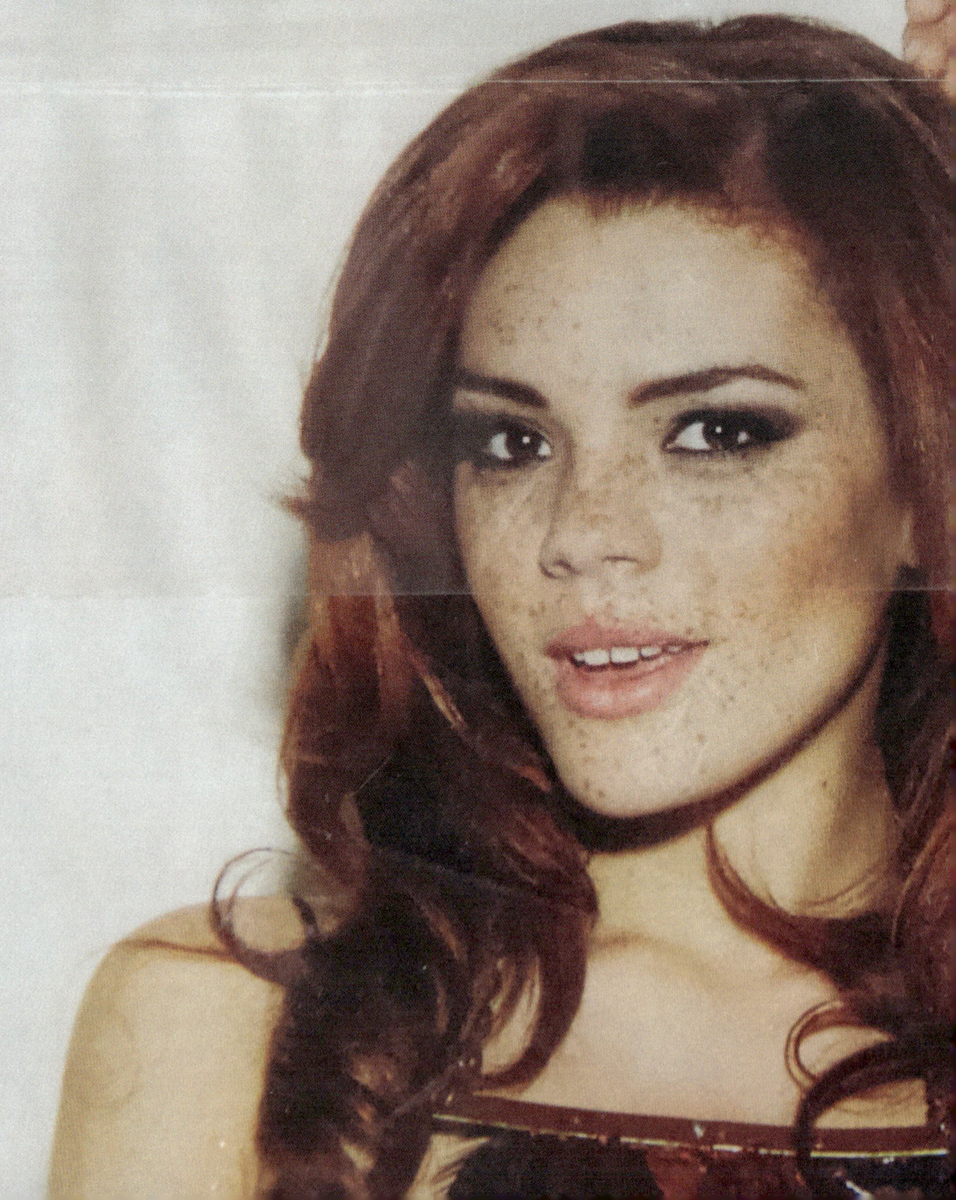

CLOTHES SHO
Fashion
AUTUMN ISSUE | clot

LIVE

Tribune

nowlive.com

Mr D Fagen
Art & Design
University Of Dundee
Queen Mother Building
Dundee
Angus
DD1 4HN   030 317   01675

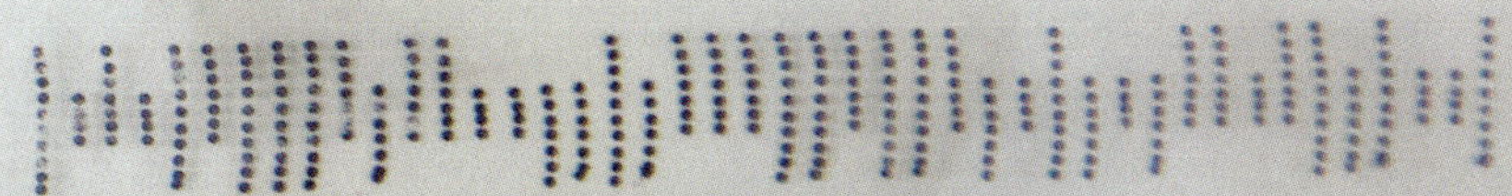

Illuminate

Private & Confidential

UNIVERSITY OF DUNDEE   831   3161776
101 02   ACADEMIC-DOJ

        G   FAGAN

FINE ART DOF J

   7000760002   <296>

PRIVATE AND CONFIDENTIAL   DO NOT DESTROY

                                            P60 Advice

PERSONAL & CONFIDENTIAL
MR G FAGAN
FINE ART
DUNCAN OF JORDANSTONE, UNIVERSITY OF DUNDEE

3161776

Private and Confidential

UNIVERSITY OF DUNDEE   831   3161776
101 02   ACADEMIC-DOJ

        G   FAGAN

FINE ART DOF J

   7000760002   <283>

25 October 2000

GRAHAM FAGAN
2/R 14 MCLENNAN STREET
MOUNT FLORIDA
GLASGOW
G42 9DQ

**SCOTTISH
NATIONAL
GALLERY OF
MODERN
ART**

BELFORD ROAD
EDINBURGH EH4 3DR
TEL: 0131-624 6200
FAX: 0131-343 2802

Dear Graham Fagan

The Trustees and Director of the National Galleries of Scotland invite you to the private view of

**Shift
new works by Alison Watt**

On
Friday 17 November 2000

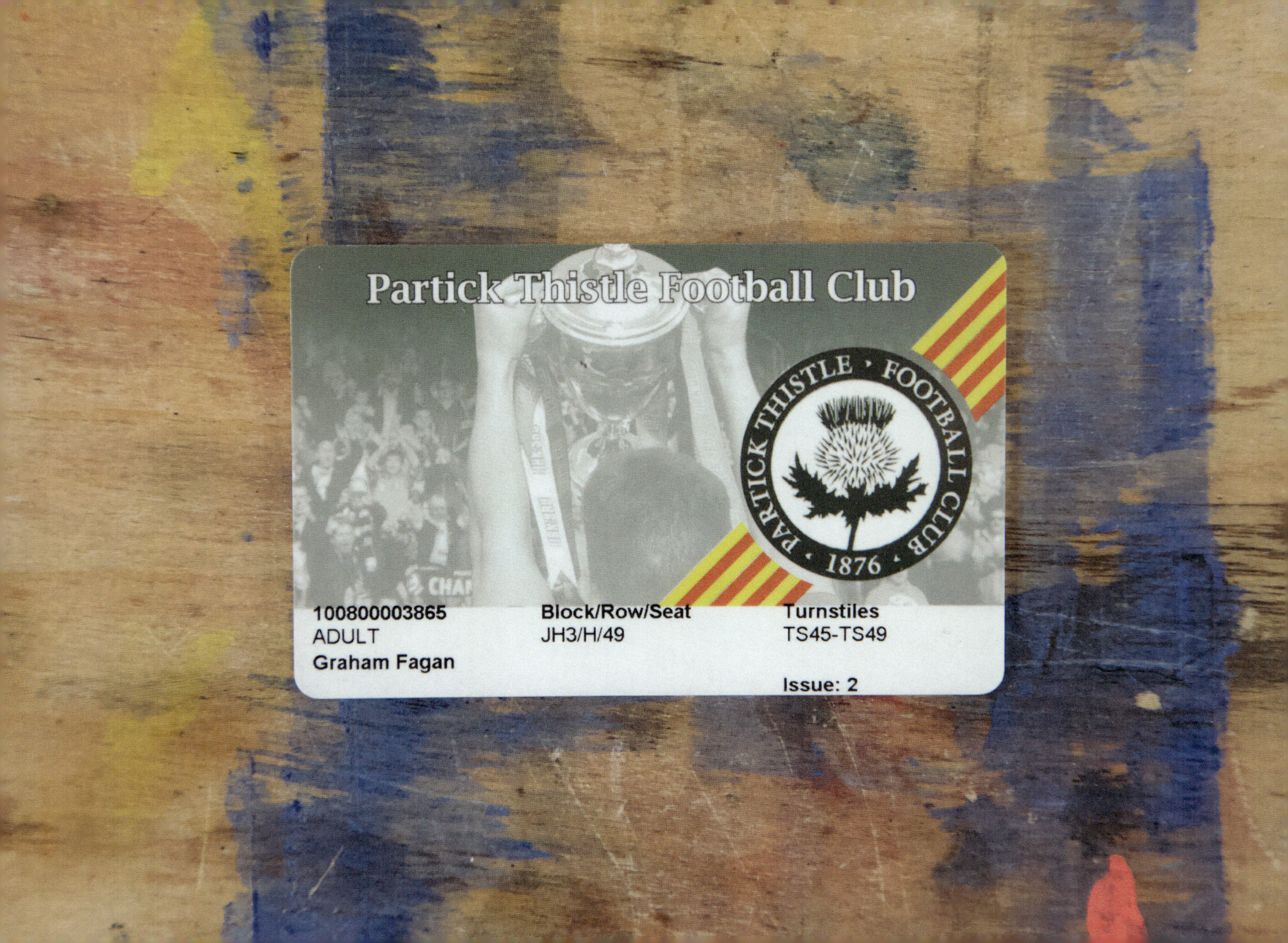

Partick Thistle Football Club
PARTICK THISTLE · FOOTBALL CLUB · 1876
100800003865
ADULT
Graham Fagan
Block/Row/Seat
JH3/H/49
Turnstiles
TS45-TS49
Issue: 2

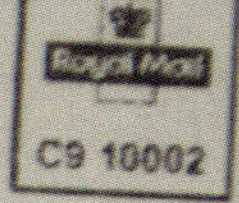

CH ... SK Unit 12
The Heathrow Estate
Silver Jubilee Way
Hounslow
Middlesex TW4 6NF

7

(ZRH)

SPA30675362

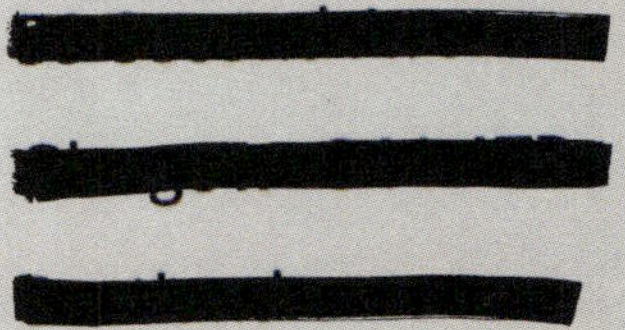

Exhibition review: RSA 187Th Annual Exhibition, Edinburgh

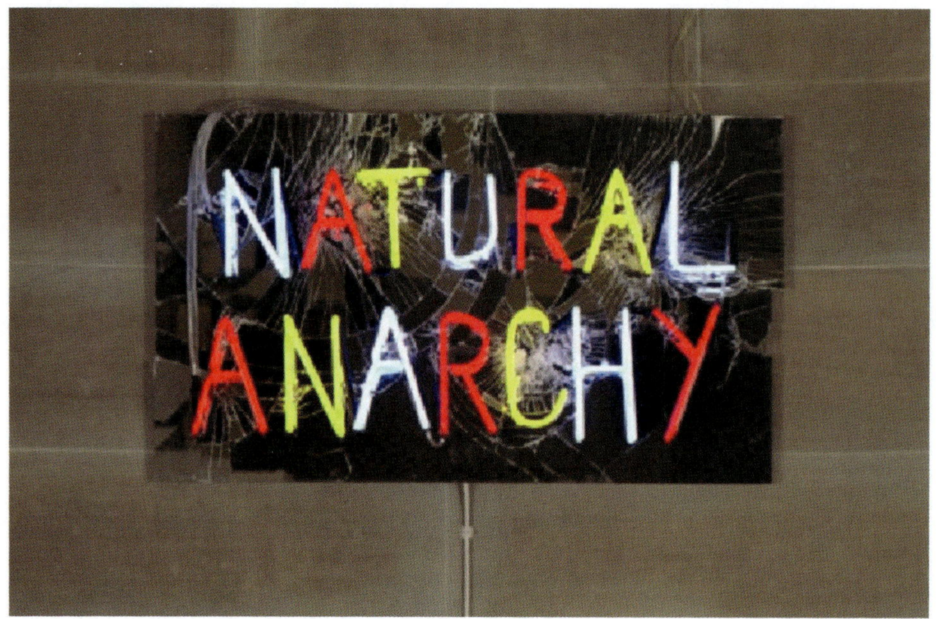

Graeme Fagen's Natural Anarchy. Picture: complimentary

By
**DUNCAN MACMILLA
N**

Published: 19:01
Wednesday 05 June 2013

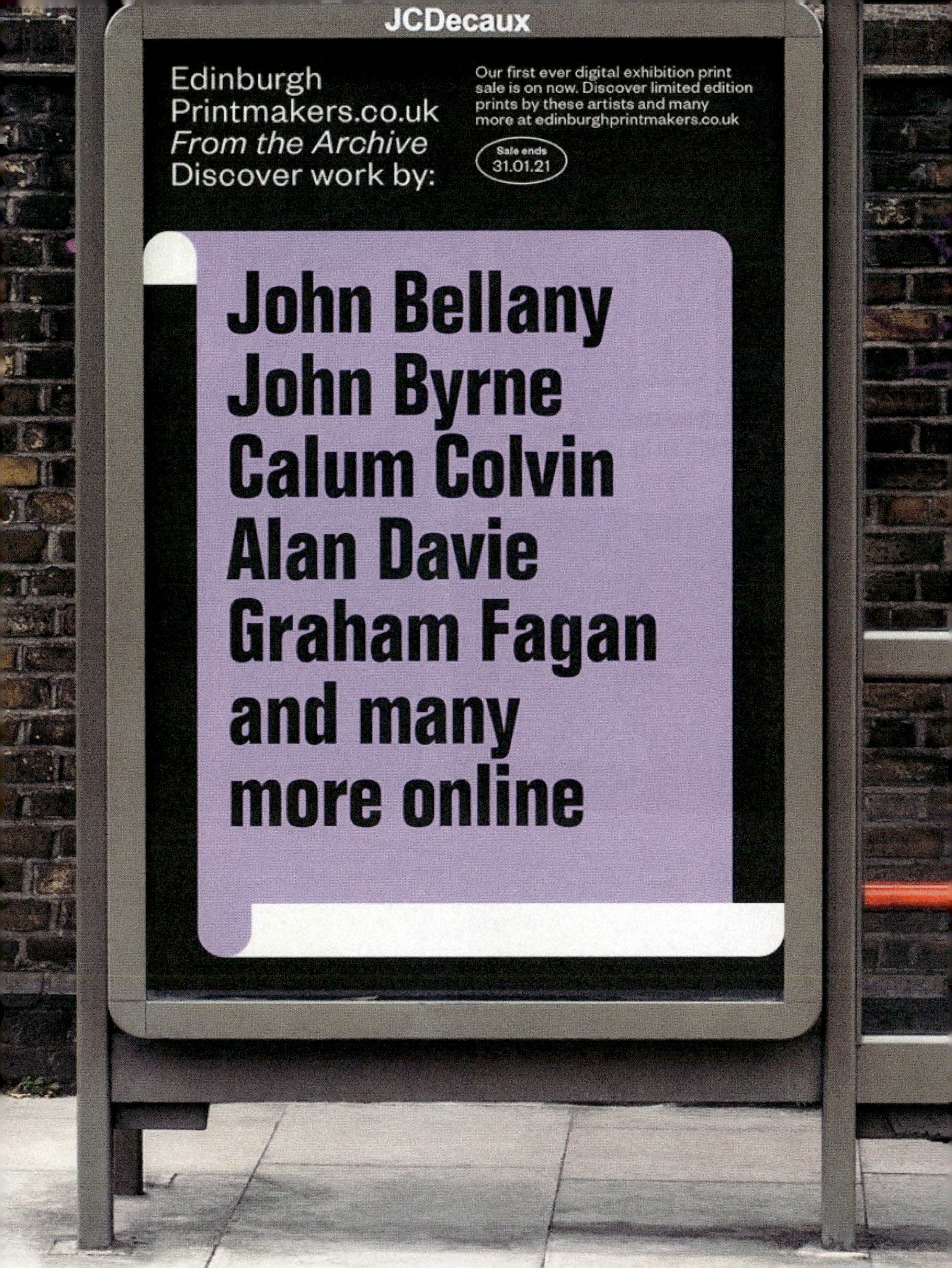

JCDecaux
Edinburgh
Printmakers.co.uk
From the Archive
Discover work by:
Our first ever digital exhibition print sale is on now. Discover limited edition prints by these artists and many more at edinburghprintmakers.co.uk
Sale ends 31.01.21
John Bellany
John Byrne
Calum Colvin
Alan Davie
Graham Fagan
and many more online

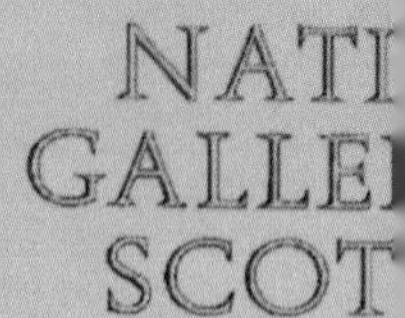

NATI
GALLE
SCOT

Simon
Director of Modern
Scottish National G
75 Belford Road · E
Phone: +44 (
Fax: +44 (0)
Email: simongroom

Graham Fagan
c/o Susanna Beaumont
doggerfisher
11 Gayfield Square
Edinburgh
EH1 3NT

10 December 2009

Dear Graham

On behalf of the Scottish National Gallery of Modern Art, I would like to thank you for your participation in **Running Time: Artist Films in Scotland 1960 to Now** this autumn at the Dean Gallery. We were thrilled to be able to present your work.

This is the first time the Gallery has dedicated an exhibition entirely to film and video, and we hope that the exhibition will be a beginning for many projects involving film in the future. The exhibition was very well received, attracting over 11,000 visitors, with many visitors returning as the programme changed over the weeks.

Thank you again for your contribution in making the exhibition such a success, and we look forward to seeing you in the Gallery very soon.

Yours sincerely,

Simon Groom
Director of Modern and Contemporary Art

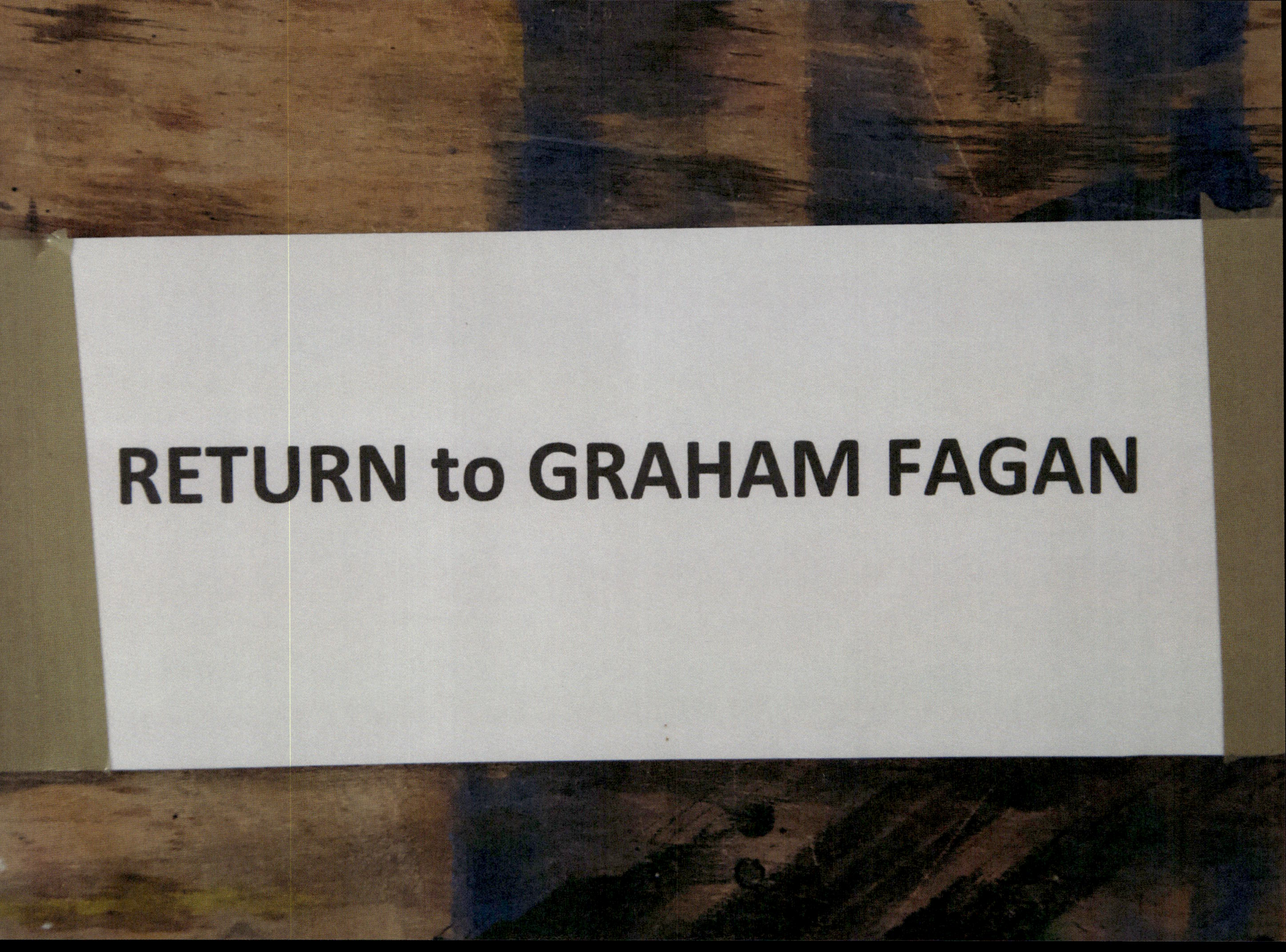

RETURN to GRAHAM FAGAN

WINTER FLOWERS

Graham Fagan RSA (Elect)
Scheme for Nature
bronze | 100 x 100 x 210cm
£8000
or ten interest free payments of £800 with Own Art

WINTER FLOWERS

Graham Fagan RSA (Elect)
Scheme for Nature
bronze | 100 x 100 x 210cm
£8000
or ten interest free payments of £800 with Own Art

WINTER FLOWERS

Graham Fagan RSA (Elect)
My Favourite Flower is the Pansy (Black)
pencil & indian ink | 29 x 39 cm
£800
or ten interest free payments of £80 with Own Art

WINTER FLOWERS

Graham Fagan RSA (Elect)
My Favourite Flower is the Pansy (Yellow and Black)
pencil & indian ink | 29 x 39 cm
£800

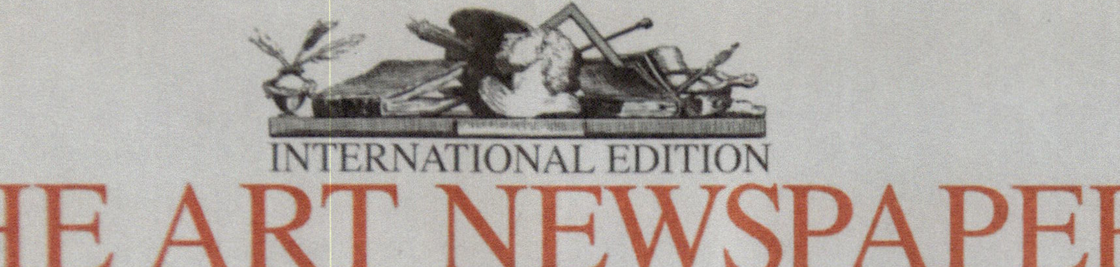

THE ART NEWSPAPER

NEWS, EVENTS, POLITICS, BUSINESS, ART, MONTHLY

ART NEWSPAPER, McGowan House, 10 Waterside Way, Northampton, NN4 7XD

Dr G Fagen
Fine Art
University Of Dundee
Duncan Of Jordanstone College Of Art And I
Perth Road
Dundee
DD1 4HT   116/11180

"Invaluable i
on internation
in the art wor

NICHOLAS SEROTA, DIRE

SUBSCRIBE TO THE ART NEWSPAPER TODAY AND

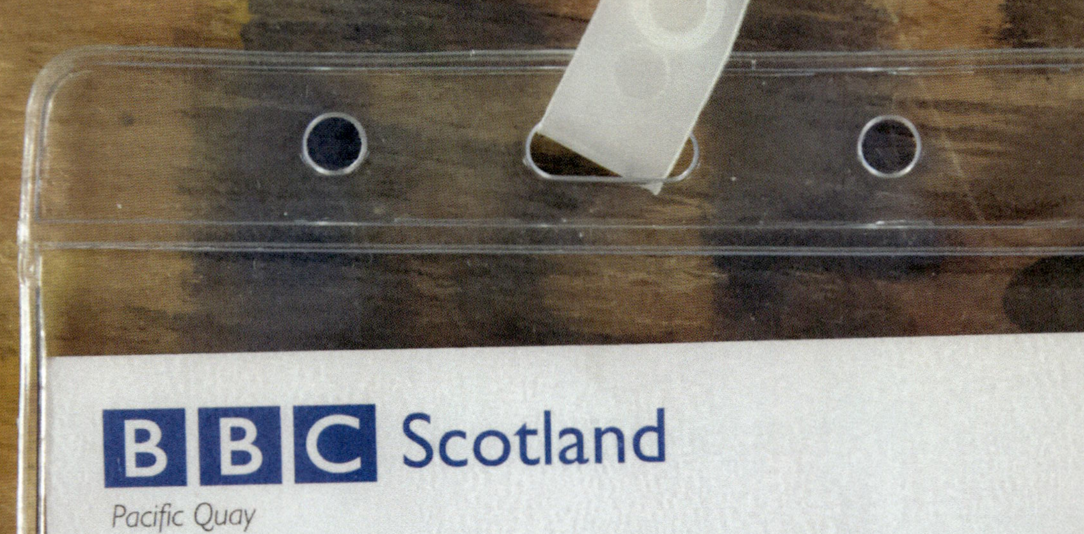

BBC Scotland
Pacific Quay
40 Pacific Quay
Glasgow
G51 1DA
Tel: 0141 422 6000
Fax: 0141 422 7912
VISITOR
GRAHAM FEAGEN
Host: Caitlin Smith
Extension:
069161
VALID UNTIL: 04/08/2015

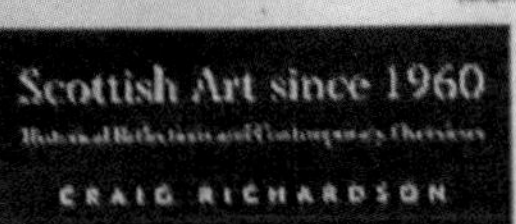
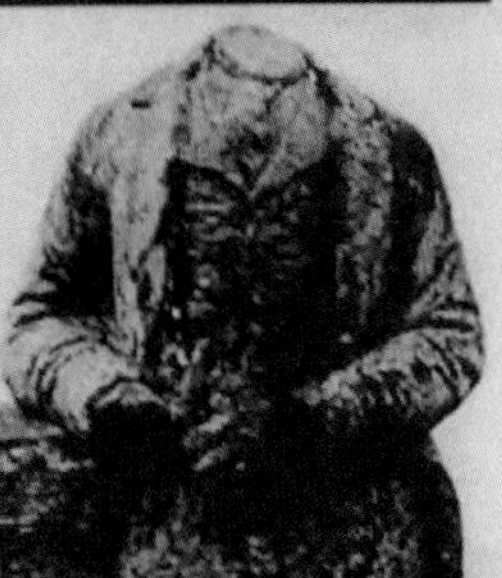

Scottish Art since 1960
Historical Reflections and Contemporary Overviews
Craig Richardson, Northumbria University, UK

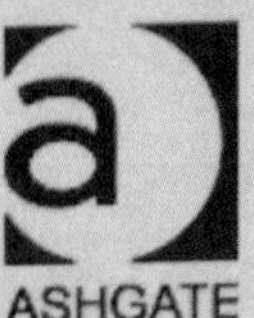

February 2011
230 pages
978-0-7546-6124-5
Includes 39 b&w illustrations

234 x 156 mm
Hardback
£65.00

Craig Richardson here addresses key areas of cultural politics and identity in a way that not only illuminates the development of Scottish art, but teases out another strand of the plurality of developments which led to the success of artists throughout the UK in the 1990s. It is of the highest relevance whether one's perspective is that of the development of the Scottish art, British art or European art of this period. The book adds significantly to our knowledge of the art of this period in a way that will aid not only our historical understanding but our understanding of the dynamics of art practice today.

Providing an analysis and including discussion (interviewing artists, curators and critics and accessing non-catalogued personal archives) towards a new chronology, Richardson here examines and proposes a sequence of precisely denoted 'exemplary' works which outlines a self-conscious definition of the interrogative term 'Scottish art.' Among the artists whose work is discussed are John Latham, Simon Starling, Alan Johnston, Roderick Buchanan, Glen Onwin, Christine Borland, William Johnstone, Joan Eardley, Alexander Moffat, Douglas Gordon, Alan Smith, Graeme Fagen, Ross Sinclair and many others. The discussion culminates in a critically original demonstration of the scope for further research and practice within the subject, facilitating national cultural debate on the character of Scottish-national visual art.

Contents
Preface; Introduction; Winter sun (1960-67); 'The feel of the situation': national identity and the avant-garde in Scottish art (1968-78); The night minds (1979-88); Rational practices (1989-2003); Bibliography; Index.

About the Author
Craig Richardson is Professor of Fine Art at Northumbria University, UK

www.ashgate.com/isbn/9780754661245

Graham Fagan

Natural Anarchy

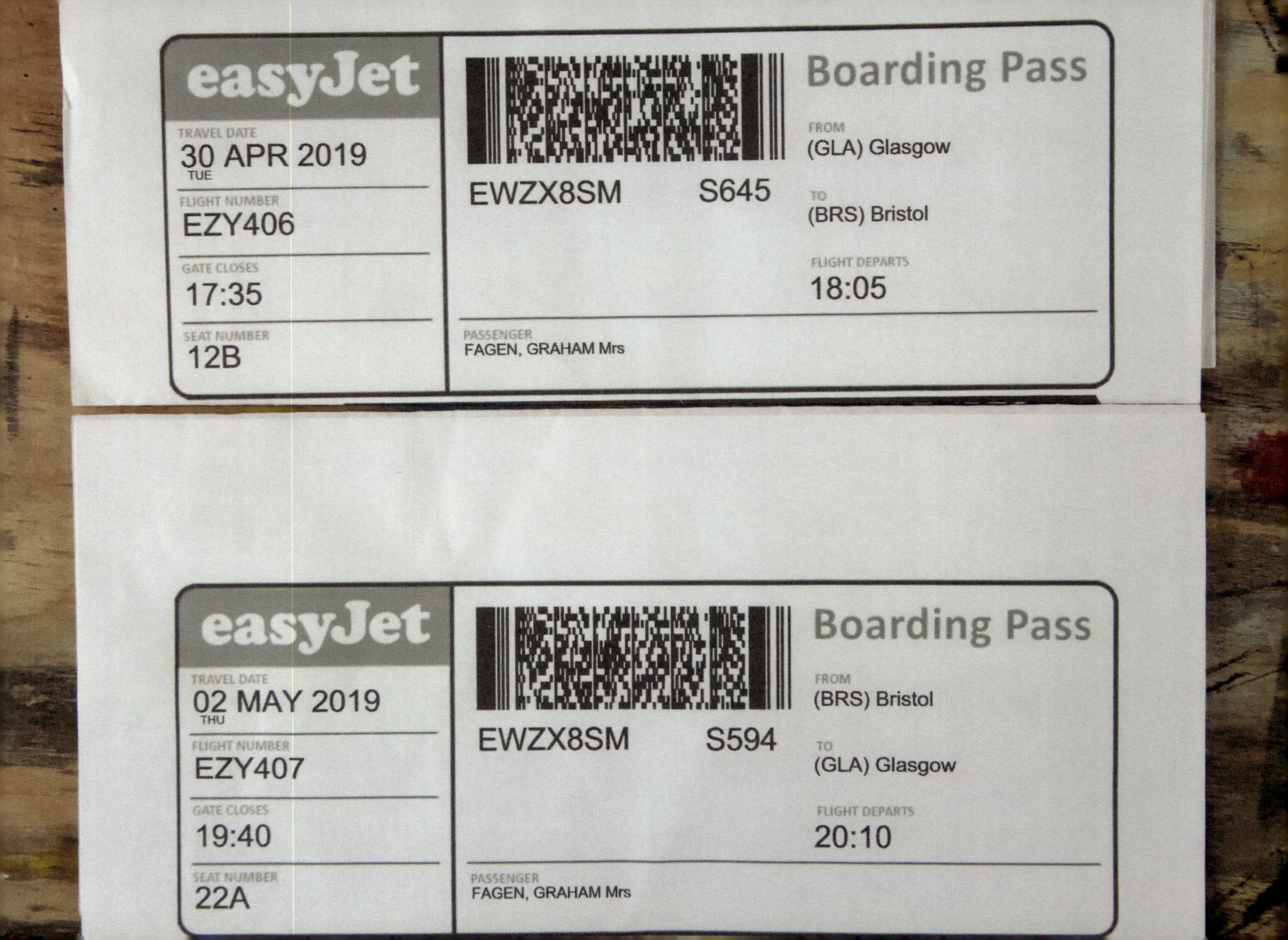

easyJet — Boarding Pass

TRAVEL DATE
30 APR 2019
TUE

FLIGHT NUMBER
EZY406

GATE CLOSES
17:35

SEAT NUMBER
12B

EWZX8SM   S645

FROM
(GLA) Glasgow

TO
(BRS) Bristol

FLIGHT DEPARTS
18:05

PASSENGER
FAGEN, GRAHAM Mrs

---

easyJet — Boarding Pass

TRAVEL DATE
02 MAY 2019
THU

FLIGHT NUMBER
EZY407

GATE CLOSES
19:40

SEAT NUMBER
22A

EWZX8SM   S594

FROM
(BRS) Bristol

TO
(GLA) Glasgow

FLIGHT DEPARTS
20:10

PASSENGER
FAGEN, GRAHAM Mrs

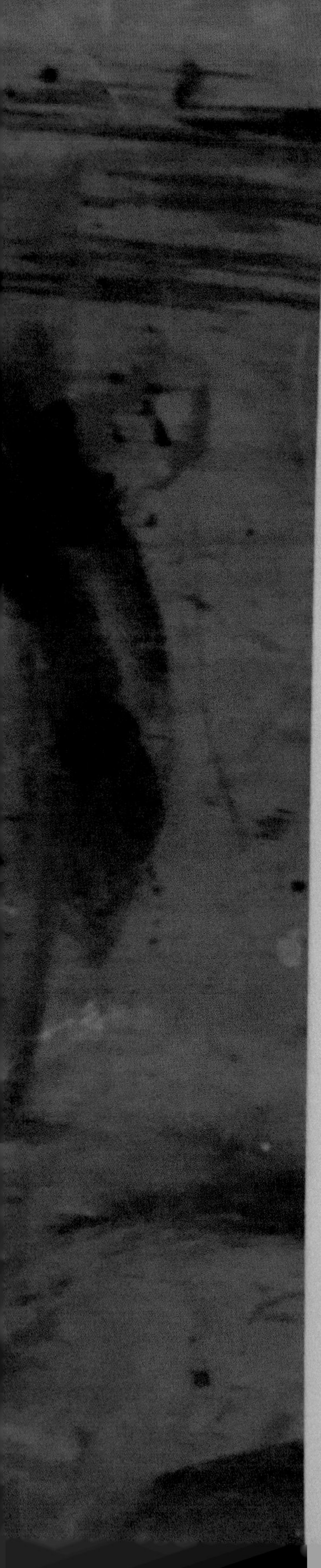

Published by William Heinemann 2013

2 4 6 8 10 9 7 5 3 1

First published in Great Britain in 2013 by
William Heinemann
Random House, 20 Vauxhall Bridge Road,
London SW1V 2SA

www.randomhouse.co.uk

Addresses for companies within The Random House Group Limited can be found at: www.randomhouse.co.uk/offices.htm

The Random House Group Limited Reg. No. 954009

A CIP catalogue record for this book
is available from the British Library

ISBN 9780434022090

The Random House Group Limited supports the Forest Stewardship Council® (FSC®), the leading international forest-certification organisation. Our books carrying the FSC label are printed on FSC®-certified paper. FSC is the only forest-certification scheme supported by the leading environmental organisations, including Greenpeace. Our paper procurement policy can be found at www.randomhouse.co.uk/environment

Printed and bound in Great Britain by Clays Ltd, St Ives PLC

For my brother, Gary Niven (1968 – 2010)

To Grahame;
the first ever 3 times
Hodge Champ.
On the occasion of
his victory.
Best
[signature] x

GRAHAM FAGAN
MISSING

**T5
13 SEPTEMBER –
2 OCTOBER 2011**

*'The police call them mispers. They are everywhere
and nowhere; in the same world and out of it; each
of them different and each the same. Mispers.'*
—Andrew O'Hagan

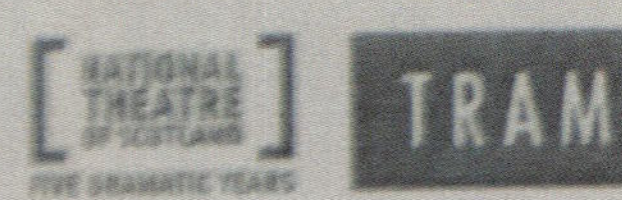

Graham Fagen is one of Scotland and the UK's foremost
artists. In video, performance, photography, sculpture o[f]
works which explore how national or personal identity is
and a response, to its cultural context.

In a major commission for the re-launch of the Scottish
Gallery on 30 November, Graham Fagen has created a ne[w]
work based on the theme of the missing; people or place[s]

Collective memory and personal responsibility, themes
Scottish National Portrait Gallery, underpin this poigna[nt]
of one of the most difficult issues we as a society have to[day]
The first screening of this new work at Tramway coincid[es]
National Theatre of Scotland's production of *The Missin[g]*
Andrew O'Hagan from his acclaimed 1995 book.

The Scottish National Portrait Gallery is delighted to be
partnership with the National Theatre of Scotland.

GRAHAM FAGAN

SCULPTURE DEPT

DUNCAN OF JORDANSTONE COLLEGE OF ART

PERTH ROAD

DUNDEE

DD1 4HT

Dear Graham Fagen,

Re. 'Petty Crimes' - Laing Gallery Touring Exhibition

The City Gallery is delighted to be showing the Laing Gallery's major touring exhibition 'Petty Crimes', from the 6th October to the 4th of November 2000.

'Petty Crimes' will bring together in Leicester, works by a number of leading national and international artists, many of whom will not previously have exhibited their work in this region. The City Gallery is one of the foremost contemporary art venues within the East Midlands and we therefore hope to attract a substantial audience for this exhibition.

As an artist exhibiting in 'Petty Crimes', we would like to welcome you to the private view to be held at the City Gallery, on Thursday 5 October, between 6.00 - 8.00pm. I have enclosed a number of invites for your personal use. If you will be able attend, then please notify us.

I hope to hear from you soon.

Yours sincerely.

Kathy Fawcett
Exhibitions Officer

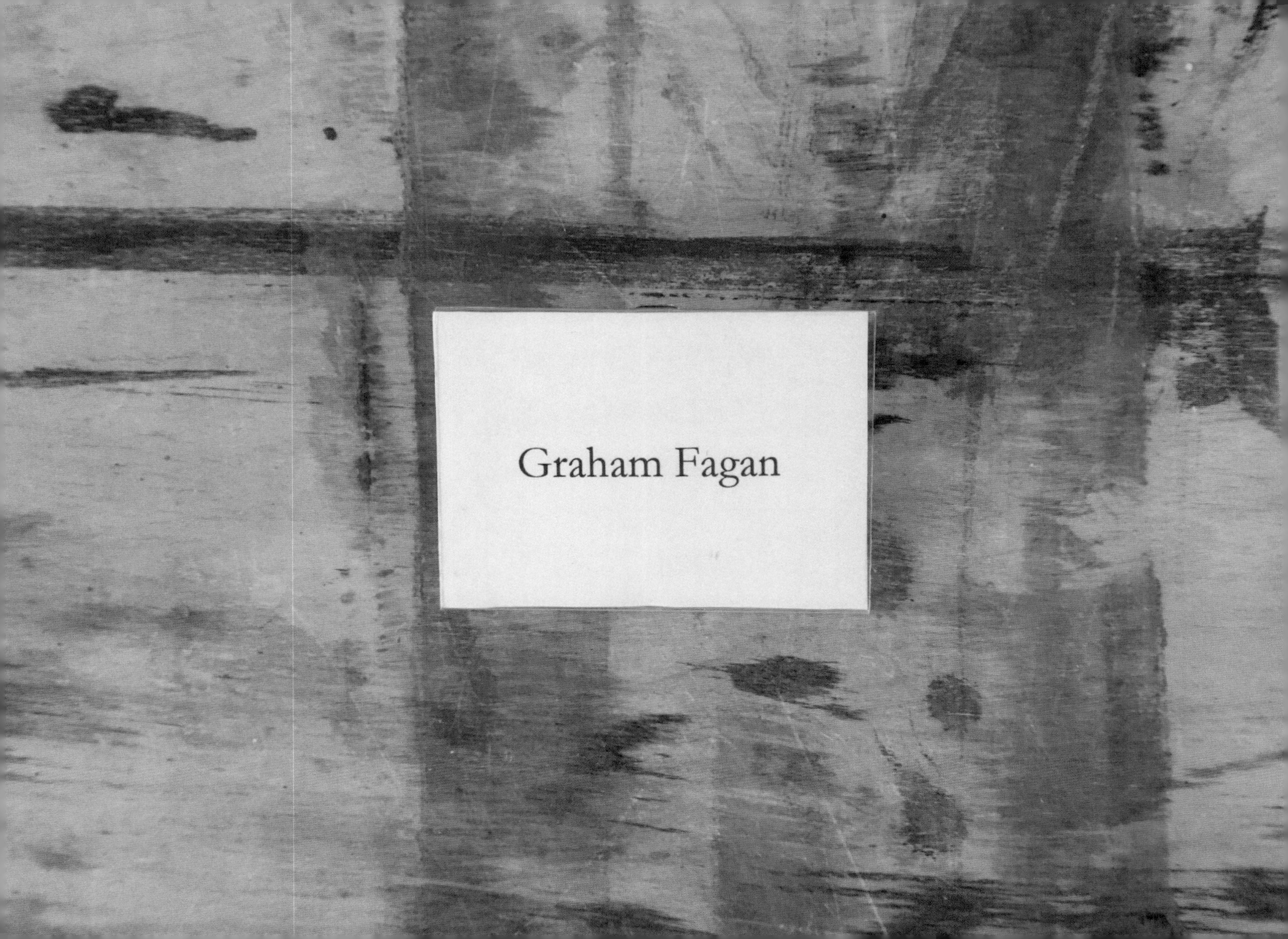

Graham Fagan

U.K. PACKING LIST

Bi

DATE 12/2/15

CUSTOMER		
Graham Gagen		

Pallets	1		CTNS.	8
WEIGHT 1	150	Kg	WEIGHT 5	
WEIGHT 2		Kg	WEIGHT 6	
WEIGHT 3		Kg	WEIGHT 7	
WEIGHT 4		Kg	WEIGHT 8	
HEIGHT 1	82 cms	M	HEIGHT 5	
HEIGHT 2		M	HEIGHT 6	
HEIGHT 3		M	HEIGHT 7	
HEIGHT 4		M	HEIGHT 8	
PICK NO.	110553			

Cartons	CONTENTS	Pallet Number	Carton Number	CONTENTS	N
1	BT8504-B x 1 / BB x 1		26		
2			27		
3			28		
4			29		
5	BT8504-B x 2 / BB x 1		30		
6			31		
7			32		
8			33		
9			34		
10			35		
11			36		
12			37		
13			38		
14			39		
15			40		
16			41		
17			42		
18			43		
19			44		
20			45		
21			46		
22			47		
23			48		
24			49		

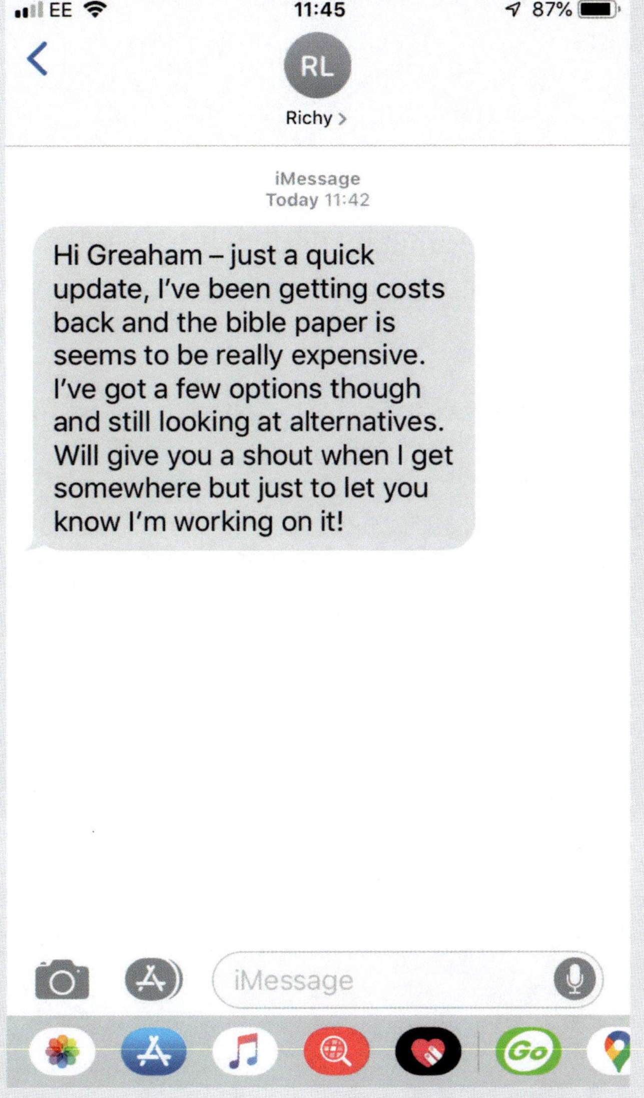

EE 11:45 87%
RL
Richy ›
iMessage
Today 11:42
Hi Greaham – just a quick update, I've been getting costs back and the bible paper is seems to be really expensive. I've got a few options though and still looking at alternatives. Will give you a shout when I get somewhere but just to let you know I'm working on it!
iMessage

11 11 1999 **Royston Road Community Parks Project**

Meeting at Landwise
Present: Landwise (George Cumberlidge, Finance Manager;
Andrew Drysdale, Project Co-ordinator, Ann Marie Doherty,
Funding Manager, Graham Smith, Construction Manager)
Fablevision, (Liz Gardiner, Yvonne Gillespie)
Visual Arts Projects (Lucy Byatt, Graham Fagin, Toby Paterson)
Loci Design (Greig White, Ian Hingley)

Purpose of meeting
Agreement on schedule from now until February when we have a Bill of
Quantity in Place

Agenda
The Next Few Months (Budgets, Contracts)

Budget
£949,000 less fees and Vat

Action: Fablevision will arrange meeting with Brian Atkinson. Landwise
will be present. It may be appropriate for Russell to attend also
n.b. Brian sits on E.T.F for New Deal and knows Landwise very well.

The next few months
To do:
a. Resolve Vat issue and decide budgets
b. Need to appoint QS (Landwise will send list of possibles)
c. R.R.P needs to contract main contractors : Landwise, Fablevision,
    V.A.P., Loci

Action a. Yvonne and Anne Marie will arrange meeting re budget. Need
to determine consultancy fees, artists residencies etc. then will know what
is available for construction. Yvonne will fax letter of award from Urban
and conditions to Ann Marie
Action: Need to be clear about what can be achieved for the reduced
money (Landwise/Fablevision).
Action: Establish system for drawing down funds. Yvonne is already in
discussion with various funders re the process of drawing down the funds
Action: Yvonne will arrange monthly claims with E.R.D.F.
Action: Lucy will ask Arts Lottery re money up front.

50/50 draw
April
1st Prize
(5)—Graham
Fagan

26th February 2019

Booking Ref. 78006160

Mr Graham Fagin

Dear Mr Fagin,

We are delighted that you have chosen to stay with us for your forthcoming visit to Bath and have pleasure in confirming the details of your reservation and ask that you check them to ensure everything is as you'd like:

Booking Reference:	78006160
Arrival Date:	Wednesday 13th March 2019
Departure Date:	Thursday 14th March 2019
Number of Nights:	1
Number of Rooms:	1
Guests:	1 Adult
Room Type:	Classic Garden View Double
Rate Per Night:	100.00 GBP
Rate Includes:	VAT, Accommodation, Parking, Breakfast

We aim to have your room available for 2pm, so if you are planning on arriving early and making the most of your time in Bath, you are very welcome to leave your luggage with us and we'll make sure it gets to your room when ready.

We would love to assist you with any dining requirements; there are over 400 restaurants in Bath and it is important to us that you have a wonderful restaurant experience during your visit. If you would just kindly advise us of your dining

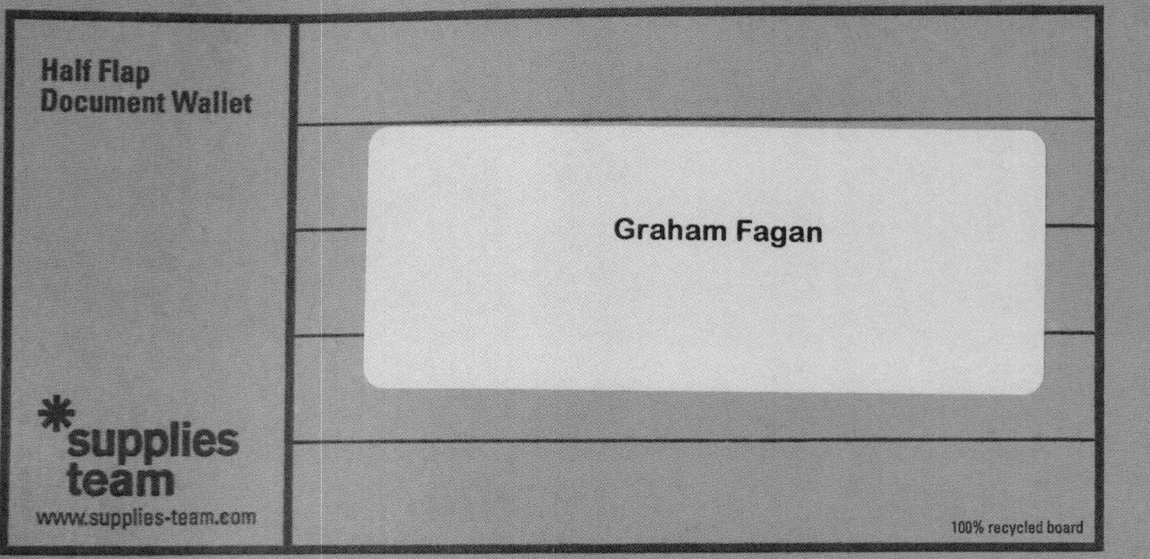

Half Flap
Document Wallet
Graham Fagan
* supplies
team
www.supplies-team.com
100% recycled board

Richard Adamson
34 Rossington Street
London
E5 8SP

Tel. 07712326101

Dear Graham Fagan,

On Sunday 10th of June, I will be holding an event called 'High Art,' as part of the
Stoke Newington Festival. Avoiding traditional methods of art dissemination and
bringing chance into the equation of receivership I will be releasing hundreds of
balloons with art works attached. Inspired by the village fete, my hope is that some of
the work will be found and that some of the recipients will reply. The event will take
place at 16.00 in Clissold Park and there will be an opportunity to see the works
before the release.

Enclosed is a clear plastic bag, which is only a suggestion on how to contain the work.
If you would like to participate please send your contribution to:

Richard Adamson,
34 Rossington Street,
London,
E5 8SP.

Please can you also supply your e-mail address or a point of contact so that I can keep
you informed of the project and the Stoke Newington Festival.
If you require any further information please contact me at the above address or at
highartuk@yahoo.co.uk

Yours sincerely,

Richard Adamson

Graeme Fagan

GRAHAM
FAGAN
TO PAU £15
DEPOSIT

MR J FAGEN
14 MACLENNAN ST.,
MOUNT FLORIDA,
GLASGOW.
G42 9DQ

GRAHAM FAGEN

Graeme Fagen

First World War Centenary

The Prime Minister

requests the pleasure of the company of

Mr Graham Fagan

at a reception at 10 Downing Street
on Tuesday 1st July 2014, from 12.30 pm to 2.30 pm

Dress: Lounge Suit
Ceremonial Day Dress

An answer is requested to:
rsvp1@no10.x.gsi.gov.uk

This invitation is not transferable

10 DOWNING STREET

Graham

Fagan

Plate

Graham Fagan
c/o Susanna Beaumont
doggerfisher
11 Gayfield Square
Edinburgh
EH1 3NT

EDINBURGH
15.12.09
GREAT BRITAIN
LP

Proof of delivery

Parcel no: **PBCD1705695001**

Your parcel was delivered on Friday 18th November 2016 at 9:33 and it was signed for by G FAGEN

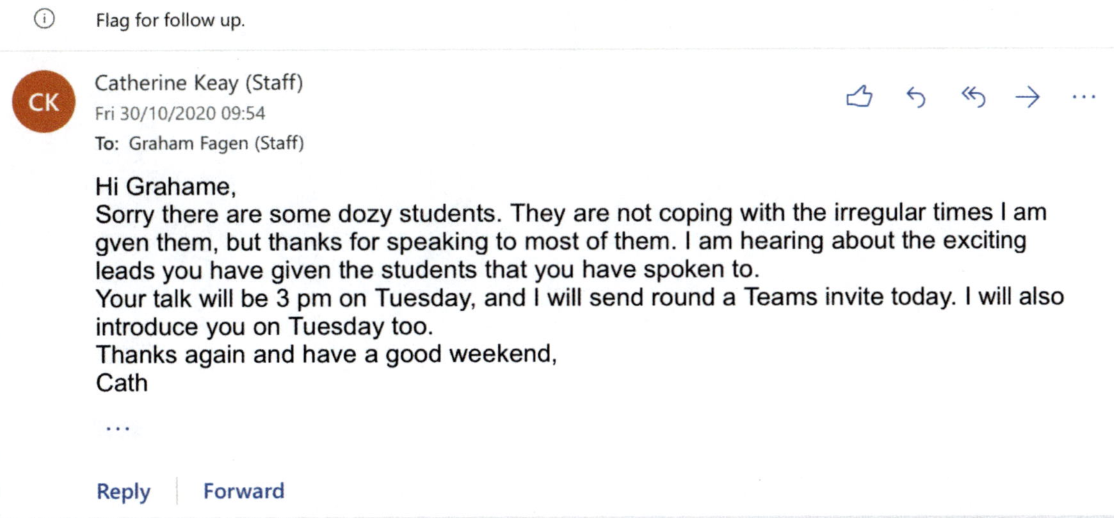

Catherine Keay (Staff)
Fri 30/10/2020 09:54
To: Graham Fagen (Staff)

Hi Grahame,
Sorry there are some dozy students. They are not coping with the irregular times I am gven them, but thanks for speaking to most of them. I am hearing about the exciting leads you have given the students that you have spoken to.
Your talk will be 3 pm on Tuesday, and I will send round a Teams invite today. I will also introduce you on Tuesday too.
Thanks again and have a good weekend,
Cath

...

Reply | **Forward**

1 Internet Message Header
2 <no topic> * Binary *

=========================== Begin Part 1 ============================
Topic: Internet Message Header

Dear Mr. Graham Fagan;

I have been trying to reach you on the mobile phone 077 12 875 466 but
cannot make contact. I have been traveling a bit throughout Kosovo or
attending meetings in Pristina, so I may have missed your calls. I be
you are in the second part of your visit for which IRC Kosovo had plan
provide you opportunities to visit villages and communities.

Could you try to contact me by e-mail since this medium seems to be mo
performing than any of the phone systems.

Best regards

Richard Jacquot

------------------------- Internet Header -------------------------
Sender: richardjacquot@yahoo.com
Received: from smtp.mail.yahoo.com (smtp.mail.yahoo.com [128.11.68.32]
    by cndmaage.compuserve.com (8.9.3/8.9.3/SUN-1.7) with SMTP id

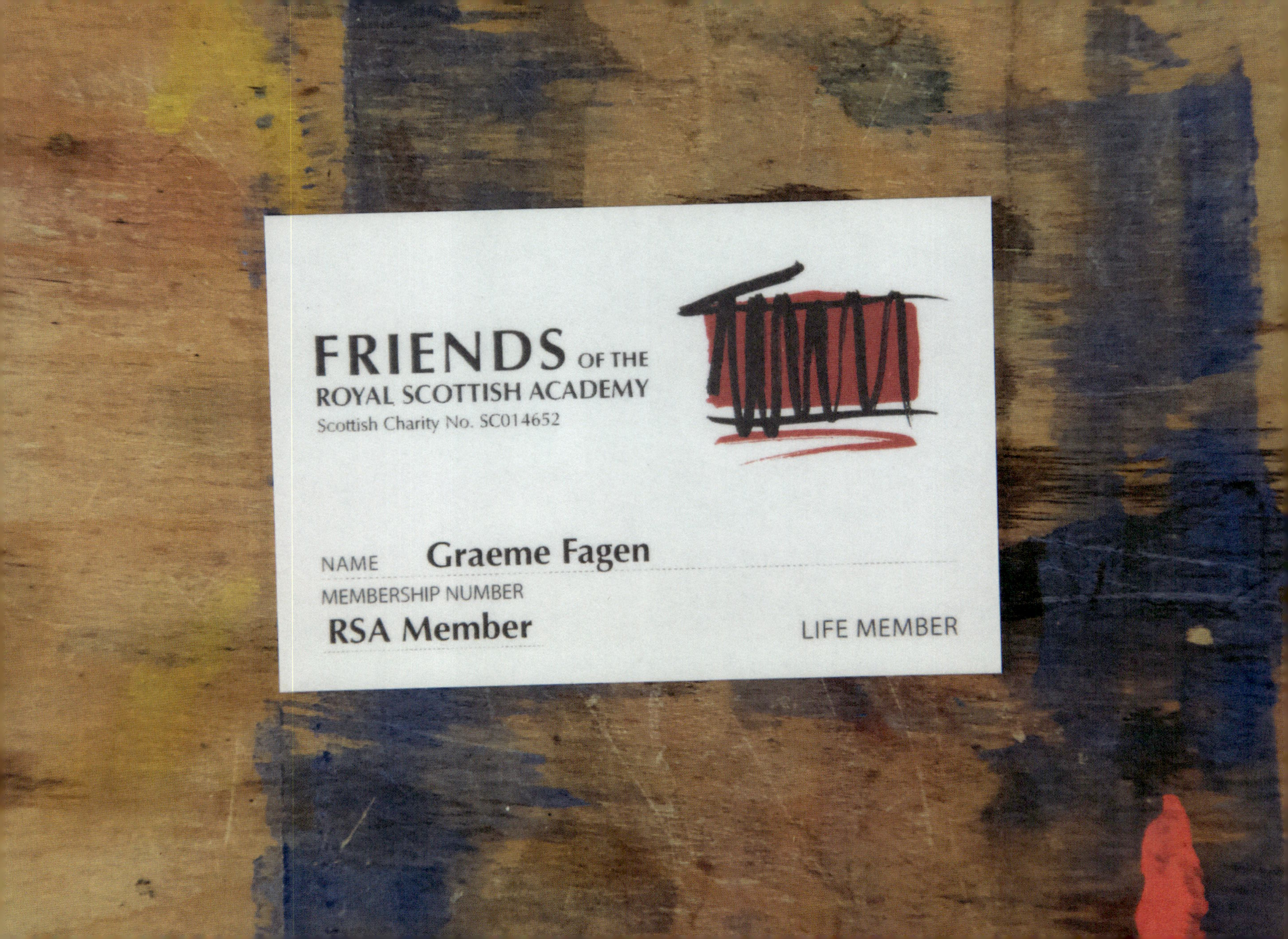

FRIENDS OF THE
ROYAL SCOTTISH ACADEMY

Scottish Charity No. SC014652

NAME **Graeme Fagen**

MEMBERSHIP NUMBER

RSA Member

LIFE MEMBER

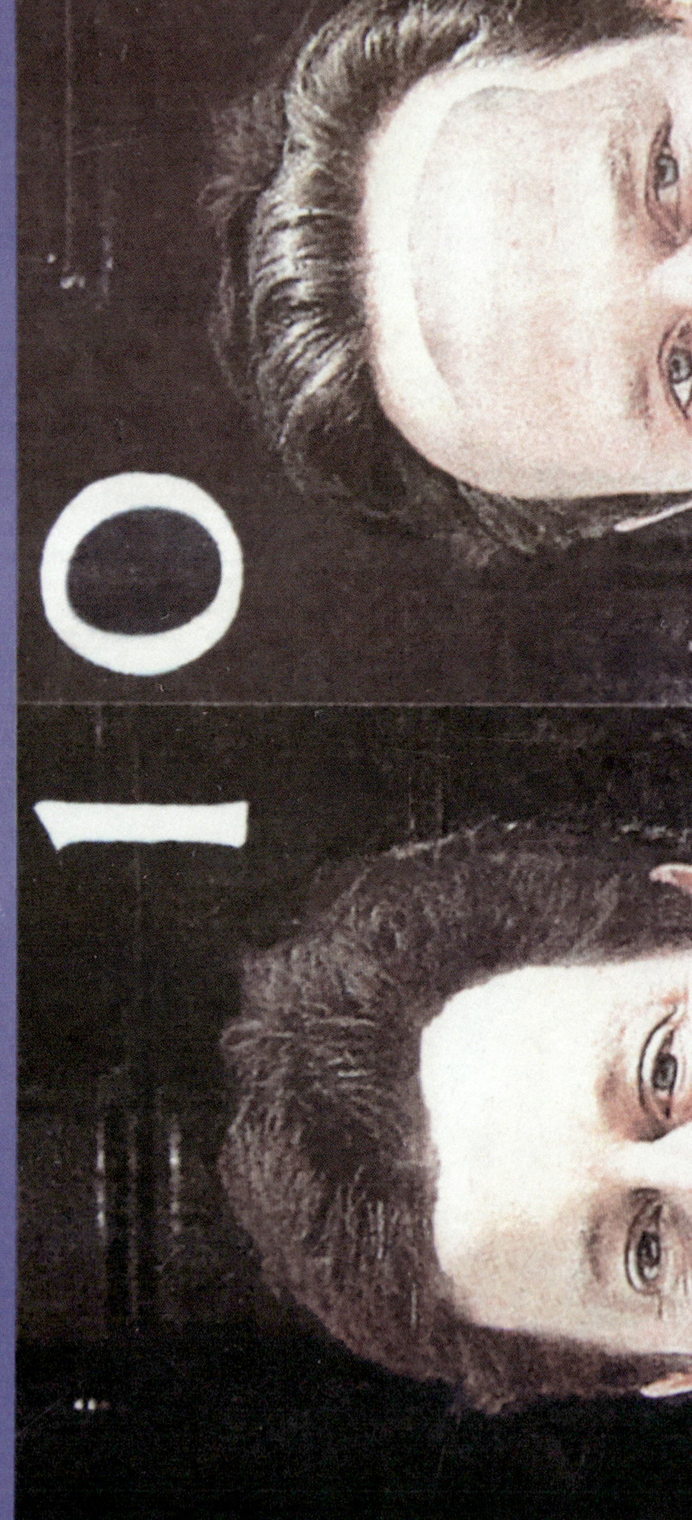

THE DROUTH

DECLINE

£4.95

10

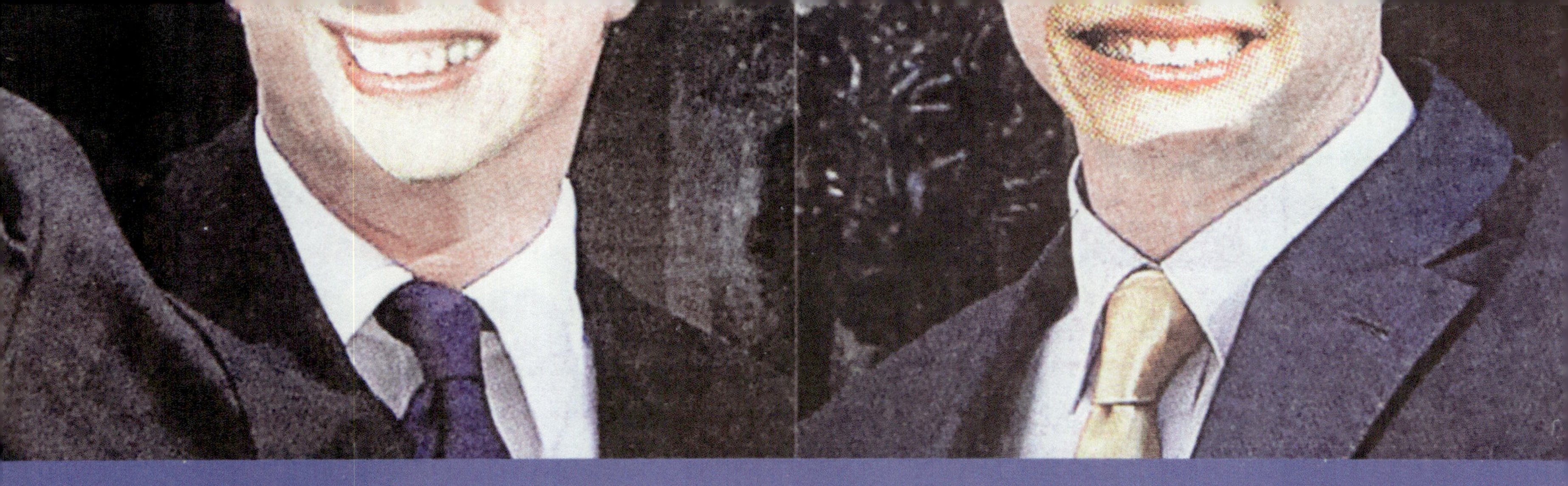

To paint - just quaint?

The Decline of Heterosexuality

Sundown with Žižek and the road to Berlin
(or Sundancing Way Out West?)

Thomas Babington Macaulay on the New Politics

Guest Artist: Graham Fagin

Guest Editor: Miriam Ross

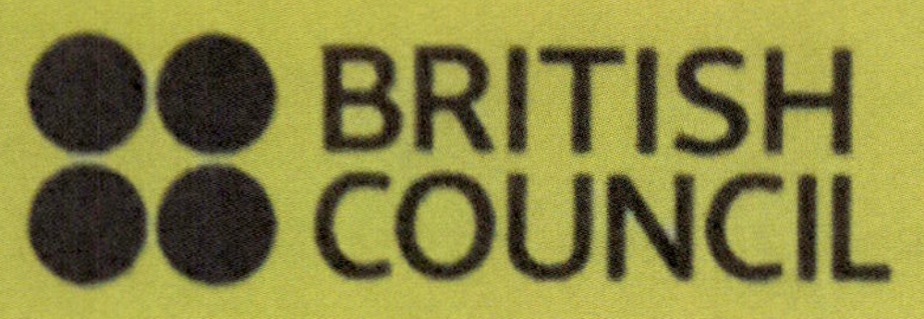

Dear Graham Fagan,

BRITISH PAVILION, GIARDINI DI CASTELLO, VENICE

Friday 8 May 13.00 – 14.00

13.15 - Welcome from Graham Sheffield CBE, Director Arts, British Council

I am delighted to invite you to an informal lunch on Friday 8 May to celebrate the many UK artists participating in the 56th Venice Biennale.

Lunch will be held in the Piano Terra of the British Pavilion in the Giardini di Castello from 13.00 to 14.00, and I very much hope that you will be able to join us.

Please let us know if you are able to attend by 28 April by contacting Myfanwy Grantham o rsvp.events@britishcouncil.org or +44 (0)20 7389 4229.

Dear Graham Fagan,

I am working with Murdo Macdonald on a revised edition of his book 'Scottish Art' to be published by Thames & Hudson as part of their 'World of Art' series in Spring 2020.

We'd very much like to include a photograph of your work for the 2015 Venice Biennale (Scotland + Venice, Palazzo Fontana, Venice, 2015) in the book.

Would you be happy for us to proceed? And if so, would you be able to supply me with a high resolution image file of the attached photograph of your work for use in the book?

I look forward to hearing from you,

Best wishes,

Pauline

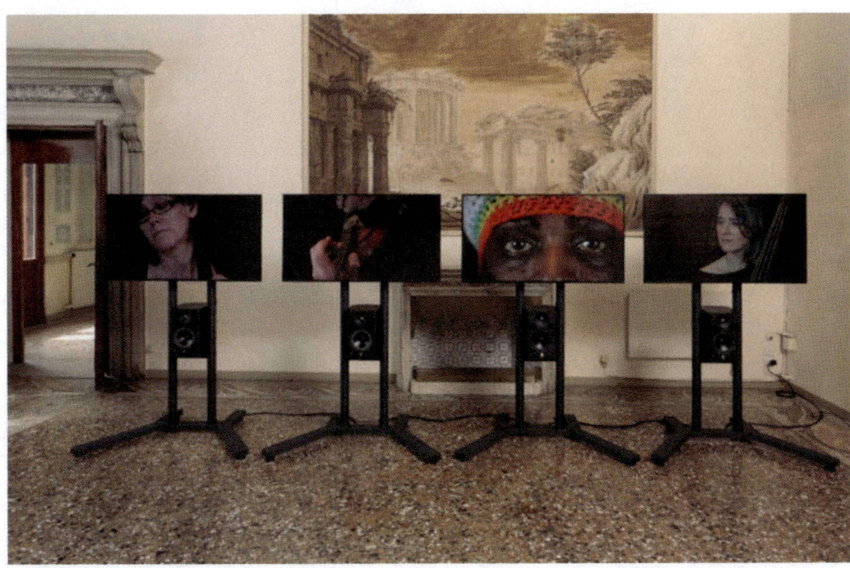

Pauline Hubner
Freelance Picture Researcher & Indexer

NEWSPAPER: KOSOVO

THEATRE

GRAHAM FAGAN

THE SCOTSMAN   News you can trust since 1817

Arts and CultureArt

Art reviews: Academicians in Isolation, RSA, Edinburgh | Great Scots in Isolation, Scottish Gallery, Edinburgh

Leading Scottish artists present work made during lockdown in two new online exhibitions at the RSA and the Scottish Gallery

By Duncan Macmillan

Saturday, 13th June 2020, 12:36 pm
Updated 23 hours ago

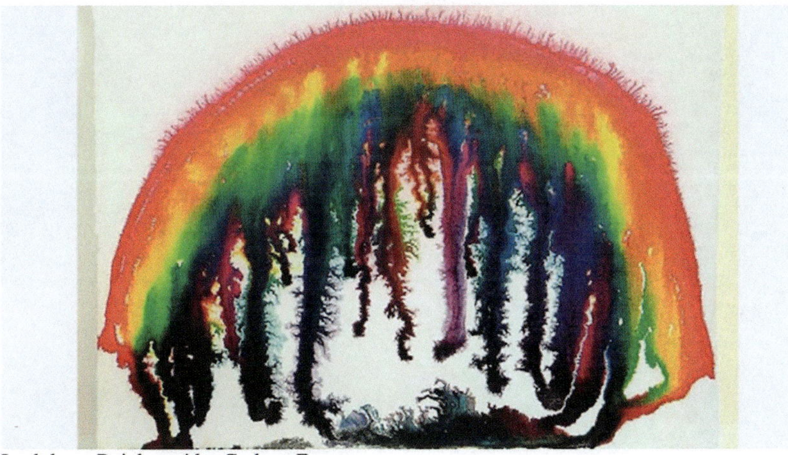

Lockdown Rainbow 4 by Graham Fagen

Academicians in Isolation, Royal Scottish Academy, Edinburgh ****

Great Scots in Isolation, The Scottish Gallery, Edinburgh ****

Graham Fagan is equally topical, painting the rainbow, symbol of solidarity against the virus. Four works in ink and watercolour have all the chromatic range of the rainbow, but the colours have run, the edges are ragged and the arc dissolved: a wry comment on our times.

From: graham fagen <graham.fagen@googlemail.com>
Date: 31 May 2011 09:30:32 GMT+01:00
To: c-andrews frac nord <c-andrews@fracnpdc.fr>
Subject: **Re: From Hilde**

Dear Christine,

I'm not Dan Graham!

The letter should be emailed to Amy Austin. Her email is aaustin@artpace.org

She may want a hard copy posted too, please ask her in your email.

Very best,
Graham Fagen

On 31 May 2011, at 07:50, c-andrews frac nord wrote:

Dear Dan Graham,
Please find the letter of introduction.
Also, could you tell me if I need to send the original to the premium processing Service (address of the letter) ?

Thanks in advance
Christine Andrews

Hilde,

thanks for getting back, there is still plenty time.

Below is the letter of introduction from Artpace and attached is the template for you to follow.
Everything should be emailed / posted back to Amy at Artpace.

Hopefully it won't take too much of your time HIlde.

Very best,
Graham

--
Christine Andrews
Assistante de Direction

FRAC Nord-Pas de Calais
Tel : 03.28.65.84.21.

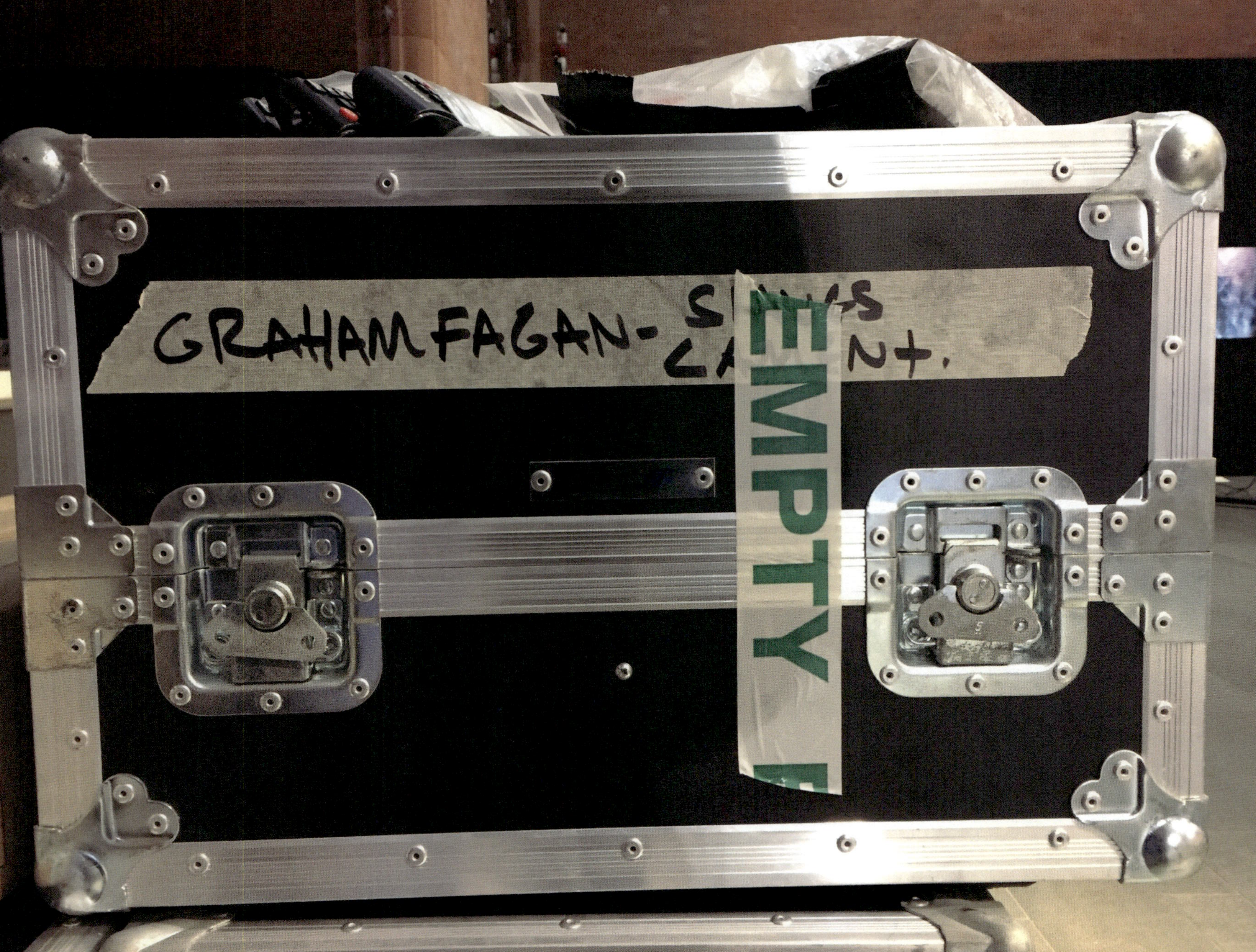
GRAHAM FAGAN - SERIES CASES +2
EMPTY
BTB504/BB
BLACK BASE WITH
BLACK POLES
BOX 2 OF 2

GRAHAM FAGAN

Graham Fagan (b. 1966) was born in Glasgow and is an acclaimed Scottish contemporary artist. Working in sculpture, drawing, photography, filmmaking, writing and text, neon, installation and performance — Fagan's work is varied and often involves him working collaboratively over extended periods of time. Fagan's work touches on the role of society and common or clashing histories through exploration of cultural turning points in the lives of both individuals and communities.

Fagan has exhibited extensively, with many solo and group shows across the globe, including; *British Art Show 5*, UK touring exhibition, *ZENOMAP*, the 50th Venice Biennale, and *Running Time*, Scottish National Gallery of Modern Art, Edinburgh. Fagan was selected to represent Scotland at the 2015 Venice Biennale.

grahamfagan.com

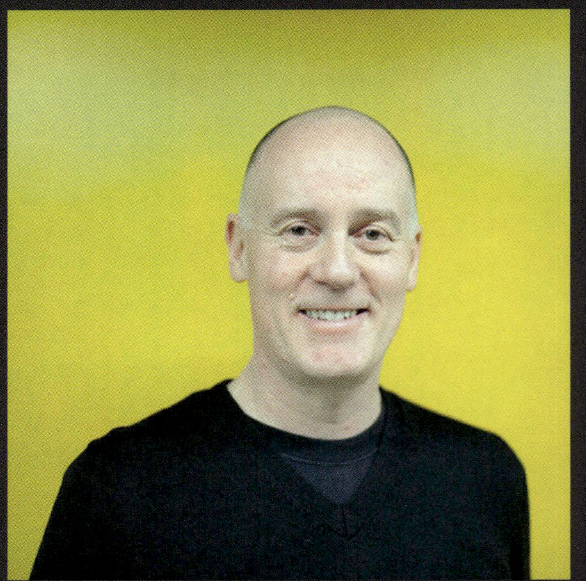

SHARE THIS PROFILE

Beginning with what remains
Sue Breakell

Encounters with artists' archives – and with the artists who create them, and who work with them – testify that to creative practitioners the archive is a place not just of recorded evidence, but of almost infinite generative potential. For artists, archives – their own, or other people's – are a rich source of material for new work, *a making-place… [that] generates unexpected questions and offers conversations for future practices*'.[1] A creative variation of the instinct that drives the historical researcher, these encounters are charged with what Hal Foster famously called an 'archival impulse'.[2] Conversations between the artist and the archive may begin in private but ultimately take public form, speaking of, and to, the wider social world.

The archive links past to present and future by being, as Nathalie Léger suggests, 'both what remains, and what begins'.[3] It is multi-layered and iterative, posing a particular set of possibilities. New work is immanent and held in the very form and matter of the archive, waiting for its day of hatching. Graham Fagen's archival impulse was honed on football cards and the bird magazine that is the earliest piece in the archive.[4] That same impulse to gather and give meaning led him to notice and to instinctively collate these misspellings, which have waited to be given a future spark of life, as they are through this exhibition and publication. The book is both a means of reflecting on what Graham has been doing all these years in collecting this stuff (the impulse), and also a look at what he has made by doing so (its product). For many years this was an impulse which hadn't yet fully declared itself, and perhaps still has much to declare, through this present making and beyond.

Because of course this archive is much more than a set of misspelt names. It is both subtle and allusive. What does it mean when we take an apparently random mistake, which recurs in many guises, and bring those incidences together and present them as a body of work? What is the nature of that accumulation as a whole, and of what does it speak? It is clearly suggestive of much more than a misspelt name: of the daily transactions of an artist's life, and of the range of contacts which these pieces in their original form bear witness to. With many different contexts to these transactions, the aggregating factor for this archive disrupts their conventional accumulation as they would appear in Fagen's wider archive of his life and work.

Clearly, any archive, being a whole of constituent parts, has its own arrangement, structure and order, as well as the potential for many others. The archive of misspellings accumulated over time in a particular way, through Graham's repeated act of gathering, but is also infinitely re-presentable in different arrangements. It has the capacity to be both a question, and the possibility of answers to questions. Away from its home life with the artist, what we see in the exhibition and the book – is a mediated archive, through the artist's intervention, operating at once as a means of allowing the archive to speak, and also as what David M Levy evocatively calls an 'act of ventriloquism'.[5] This project takes a particular view on an already subjective document set. Transmuted into a series of images, the material variations of the archive's pieces – the paper, the visual forms it carries, the handwriting or the printed text, the placing of a computer-generated label – have been flattened. As well as the partial erasure of their formats, small documents are made bigger, and bigger documents made smaller, regardless of their original status. The work, and the archive from which it is indissoluble, match the writer Christian Prigent's description of the creative process as 'the labour of transforming a documentary material into something else, which erases it, while keeping its *spectre*'.[6]

The archive also speaks of the formalities of documentary exchange and written communication: of all the ways that an artist is addressed and labelled. It is a kind of malfunctioning index of text-based transactions: the formality of an exhibition loan request, the ephemeral functionality of a visitor pass; the expired usefulness of an empty envelope. Does it matter if it's misspelt, if the communication reaches its destination, if the transaction still works? Does it even make sense as a set, if it doesn't match, except in its unifying principle of being 'wrong'. Internet and library/archive catalogue searches alike are testament to the perils of a name being spelt wrong – you may not be found, and in the digital world, visibility is all. Legal rights can't be proved if the name doesn't match: but many of these items record more humdrum transactions than the exercise of a legal entity. Is it still Graham Fagen's archive, if the name isn't right? Of course: because the very shaping of this set reveals that the unifying force is the artist, and his identities both public and private, and that this is carried in more than words on paper.

The tracing of family history tells us that, in fact, spelling of names has always been fluid over time. The etymology of names from earliest times was a move to a specificity that allowed the identification of an individual – to a kind of person-label. This system carries within it the propensity for variation, through the fallibility and the inventive interpretive responses of the humans who employ these person-labels. As such, these images are strangely familiar to us all.

Sue Breakell is Archive Leader and Senior Research Fellow at the University of Brighton Design Archives.

1   Paul Clarke, Simon Jones, Nick Kay and Johanna Hinsley (2018) 'Introduction': inside and outside the archive' in *Artists in the Archive: Creative and Curatorial Engagements with Documents of Art & Performance*. Abingdon (Oxon): Routledge.

2   Hal Foster (2004) 'An Archival Impulse', *October* 110.

3   Nathalie Léger (2012) introduction to the series 'Le lieu de l'archive', *Supplément à la Letter de L'Imec* (Paris: Institut Mémores de l'édition contemporaine). This introduction appears in all the books in the series, including Prigent (below).

4   Breakell and Fagen decided to leave inconsistencies in use of the artist's forename and surname as they appeared in the original draft of this piece.

5   David M Levy (2001) *Scrolling Forwards: Making Sense of Documents in the Digital Age*. New York: Arcade Publishing.

6   Christian Prigent (2012), *L'archive e(s)t l'œuvre e(s)t l'archive*, *Le Lieu de l'Archive. Supplément à la Letter de L'Imec* (Paris: Institut Mémoires de l'édition contemporaine). My translation. The book's title in French elides both 'is' and 'and' in the form 'e(s)t': the archive is/and the work is/and the archive'.

Ping Pong Club
Preamble to the exhibition of the archive of the misspelling of Graham Fagen.

I tried to join a ping-pong club
Sign on the door said "all full up"
I got nicked, fighting in the road
The judge didn't even know
What's my name, name, name

What's My Name, The Clash
Songwriters: Strummer / Jones / K. Levine*
Lyrics © Universal Music Publishing Group

—

I first became aware that my name was difficult for other people to spell and remember when I was in the Scouts, aged 11. I was a Cub Scout. The wee troop. The one you're in before you join the big, proper, Scout troop.

A Cub Scout leader woman, who we had to refer to as Akela, would read out loud a register at the start of each Cub Scout night.

Akela is anyone who acts as a leader to the Scout. In Cub Scout packs, Akela is a symbol of wisdom, authority, and leadership. Sir Robert Baden-Powell, the founder of the Scouting movement, chose Rudyard Kipling's The Jungle Book as a source of symbolism and allegorical framework for the youngest members of the Scouting movement. Kipling obtained the name *Akela* from Hindi, meaning *alone*.

The formality of the register started off fine, probably because I had to tell Akela my name and spell it when I joined.

"Graham Fagen?" said Akela reading out the register.
"Here!" I replied.

Then, over the following weeks, Akela started to struggle.

"Graham Fajen?" she said with her eyes squinting at the register.

"Here – but it's Graham Fagen" I offered.

Over the weeks she would default back to *"Fajen?"* After a few weeks of me correcting Akela, I gave in. I stopped replying. I stopped correcting the mispronunciation and was marked absent. I was there but I wasn't.

She kept reading out the register. I would hear what was supposed to be me and stayed silent. I developed into a sort of *"Fajjin?"* which quickly advanced on to something like *"Fadjin?"* and then, to emphasise our Scottishness perhaps, I was *"McFadjin?"*

Just before I chucked the Cub Scouts I approached Akela one last time to tell her I wasn't on the register.

"We can't have that" she proclaimed.
"Now, what's your name?"

* *Keith Levene was a founding member of The Clash. Although he left the band before the debut LP was recorded, he co-wrote the song What's My Name with Joe Strummer and Mick Jones. In a strange coincidence with Graham Fagen's archive collected in this book, Levene's credit on the back cover of The Clash LP is misspelled.*

Glasgow
International
2020

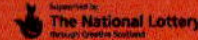

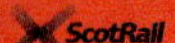

Published by Matt's Gallery to accompany *Ping Pong Club: An exhibition of the archive of the misspelling of Graham Fagen* at Queens Park Railway Club, as part of Glasgow International, 11–27 June 2021.

Graham Fagen would like to thank all the misspellers of his name as well as Queens Park Railway Club, Matt's Gallery and Duncan of Jordanstone College of Art & Design.

Sue Breakell is Archive Leader and Senior Research Fellow at the University of Brighton Design Archives.

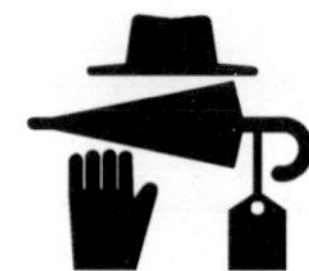

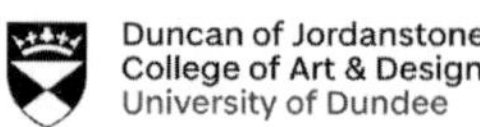

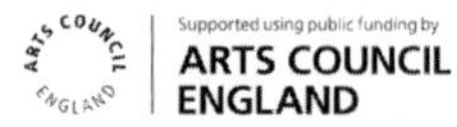

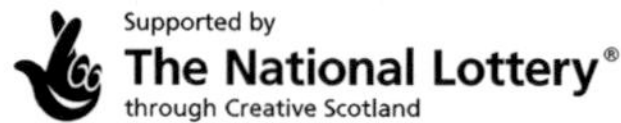

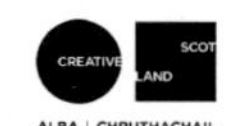

Matt's Gallery, Bermondsey
92 Webster Road, London SE16 4DF
020 7237 0398
info@mattsgallery.org
mattsgallery.org

Director: *Robin Klassnik OBE*
Deputy Director: *Tim Dixon*
Artists & Exhibitions Assistant: *Alice Cocks*
Gallery Assistant: *Chloe Carroll*
Bookkeeper: *Sophie Luard*
Board of Trustees: *Darryl de Prez (Interim Chair), Jes Fernie, David Field, Marcelle Joseph, Robin Klassnik, Matthew Krishanu, Nayia Yiakoumaki*

Special thanks to our:
Founding Benefactors: *Ron & Deborah Law Henocq, James & Jennifer Esposito*
Founding Patrons: *Charlotte & Alan Artus, Darryl de Prez & Victoria Thomas, Elinor Jansz & Alex Sainsbury, Marcelle Joseph, Dan Salmon, Dorthe Steffensen, Christopher Turner*
Friends: *Stephen Bury, Jeremy Cooper, Clare Fitzpatrick, Karen Knorr, Henry Meyric-Hughes, Bruce Stinson; Christoph & Marion Trestler*
and those who wish to remain anonymous.

Matt's Gallery is a registered charity.
Registered Charity No.1169683
Registered Company No.10231860

Queens Park Railway Club
492 Victoria Rd, Glasgow G42 8PQ
contact@queensparkrailwayclub.co.uk
queensparkrailwayclub.co.uk

Queens Park Railway Club is an artist run space located on the platform of Queens Park Railway Station on the South side of Glasgow. Run by Patrick Jameson and Ellis Luxemburg, the space has a continuing programme of events including exhibitions and residencies for artists and writers.

Queens Park Railway Club is an incorporated body with charitable status (SCIO) SC.046131

Designed and typeset by Richy Lamb

ISBN: 978-1-912717-09-5

With support from Duncan of Jordanstone College of Art and Design, University of Dundee, Creative Scotland and Arts Council England.